a lamp in every corner

a lamp in every corner

Our Unitarian Universalist Storybook

Janeen K. Grohsmeyer

UNITARIAN UNIVERSALIST ASSOCIATION
BOSTON

Printed in the United States of America
Text and cover design by Kathryn Sky-Peck

ISBN 1-55896-473-8

07 06 05 04
5 4 3 2 1

For the wording of the seven Principles in the "What We Believe" section, we are grateful to
Carol Holst and the Unitarian Universalist Church of the Verdugo Hills in California.

To my children,

Ryan and Irene,

who were the first to ask me to tell a story,

and in memory of

Sophia Lyon Fahs,

educator, author, minister, and storyteller.

Contents

W HAT W E B ELIEVE: *Seven Stories of UU Principles*

Introduction

In many Unitarian Universalist congregations, several minutes at the beginning of the worship service are reserved specifically for the children. This time may be referred to as the Children's Sermon, a Time for All Ages, Generation to Generation, the Sharing Moment, the Family Story, or some other name. It usually lasts about five minutes, and it may happen every week or once a month. It might be held either in front of the entire congregation or in the Children's Chapel.

The children's time also varies in content and form. It is sometimes a mini-sermon or a question-and-answer session conducted by the minister or by the director of religious education. It might be a song performed by the children themselves, a dance for everyone, or a skit performed by the youth. Often, an adult reads a story aloud from a book. But sometimes a storyteller shares a tale.

A storyteller can bring a different flavor and feel to a tale than a book reader can. Children like stories both ways, of course, but oral stories are far more ancient than books. For countless thousands of years, people have told each other stories of their history and their culture. However, with the advent of widespread literacy, and of television, videos, audiotapes, computer games, and other modern media, storytelling has become rare.

Yet children still like stories, and they learn easily from stories. While many stories carry morals that are appropriate for a church setting, it is important that we also pass along our UU history and culture. This book was written to help teachers, parents, and ministers do just that.

Each of the twenty-one stories in this book is about Unitarian Universalism. The first set of seven stories is about events in UU history. The second set is about famous Universalists and Unitarians. The third set illustrates the seven Principles. The first two sets are historical, about real people and real events. While details and descriptions may be changed, the basic facts should not be altered, or our understanding of our history will be confused. The third set is written in a folktale style and may be adapted in any fashion. The section, "How to Tell a Story and Create a World," at the end of this book gives suggestions on how to create stories and tell them in front of an audience.

The stories were designed to be told aloud in front of the entire congregation in about five to eight minutes. However, some aspects of some stories may be confusing or unfamiliar to very young children. Worship leaders and teachers should be prepared to answer questions or explain things further. Additional historical information follows many of the stories, for use in expanding the story or for discussion in class. Links to UU curricula lessons that focus on the historical events or the people are also listed.

The stories were written from an American viewpoint in 2004. Poland is "across the sea," references are made to United States history, American states and cities are mentioned by name, and the flaming chalice was drawn "more than sixty years ago." Feel free to change these details as necessary. Instead of mentioning the time "when there were only twenty-four stars on the American flag," you could say "when George IV was on the throne of England," or give another detail that best suits your audience and your locale. Subtract 1941 from the current year to find out how old the flaming chalice is. Make the stories yours, so you can share them with the children.

These twenty-one stories are not meant to be a comprehensive history or summation of UU values. Many more stories remain to be told.

How We Came to Be

Seven Stories of UU History

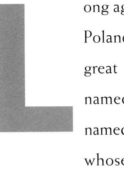

1568

A Unitarian King

Long ago, far across the sea in the country of Poland, a land of wind-swept plains and great flowing rivers, there lived a king, named King Sigismund, and a queen, named Queen Bona. They had a daughter, whose name was Princess Isabella. As Isabella grew, the king and the queen taught her to be a good and wise ruler over all of the people in the land.

When Princess Isabella was grown, a king from a neighboring country asked for her hand in marriage, and her parents said yes. Isabella was excited to be marrying King John of Hungary, until she realized that she would have to leave home.

"I shall miss you, Mother," Isabella said, suddenly wishing that she did not have to go.

"And I shall miss you," her mother replied. "But some of your friends are going with you, and if you ever have need, I will send my good friend Dr. Biandrata to you. He will watch over you if you are ill, and he will give you counsel when you are well." Her father kissed her on the forehead, and her mother kissed her on the cheek, saying, "Go with God, my daughter, and be a good wife to your new husband, and a wise queen of your new land, as we have taught you to be."

And so, with her parents' blessing and with her friends by her side, Isabella set out with a glad heart and a strong will, determined to be a good wife to her new husband, and a wise queen of her new land.

The wedding was glorious, and Princess Isabella of Poland became Queen Isabella of Hungary. And soon, Isabella had another title, for she gave birth to a little boy, and she became a mother as well as a queen. They named the little boy John Sigismund, after his father, King John of Hungary, and after his grandfather, King Sigismund of Poland.

Isabella wanted to be a wise and good queen, and to help all of the people, but the land of Hungary was torn by great wars. The king fought with other kings. The nobles fought with each other. This group of people fought with that group of people, and those people fought with these. Everywhere, people complained about taxes, they argued about religion, and they fought about land. Sometimes they fought about simply getting enough to eat. They fought and they fought and they fought, and many people died.

Isabella's husband was away fighting when their baby was born. "Come home," she wrote to him. "Come home and see our son." But King John became sick and died when their baby was only two weeks old, and he never saw his son.

The nobles elected the baby prince as their new king and cried, "All hail King John Sigismund of Hungary!" But young King John was much too young to rule a country torn by war. Other kings from other countries took most of Hungary away from John and kept it for themselves. Isabella and young John ended up living in a small eastern corner of the kingdom, a place beyond the forests, a grassy plain surrounded by high mountains and watered by quick, rushing streams, a land called Transylvania.

And there, in the only corner of the kingdom that was left to them, Isabella lived with her son, John, and with her mother's friend Dr. Biandrata. As John grew, Isabella and Dr. Biandrata taught him, as Isabella's parents had taught her, to be a good and wise ruler over all of the people in the land.

But the wars didn't stop while John was growing up. The people were still fighting, sometimes with other countries, sometimes with each other. They still complained about taxes, and they still argued about religion. Different people followed different religions in Transylvania, and none of them seemed to get along. The Catholics were arguing with the Lutherans, the Lutherans were arguing with the Greek Orthodox, the Greek Orthodox were arguing with the Calvinists, the Calvinists were arguing with the Catholics . . . it just went on and on and on.

In 1557, Queen Isabella issued a new law in the name of her son the king. The law said that people could talk about and discuss religion, but they must not argue—and certainly never fight—about religion anymore.

Two years later, Isabella died. John was nineteen. Now he had to rule by himself. He wanted to be a wise and good king, and to help all the people, just as his mother had tried to do, but the people were still arguing about religion.

"What should we do?" young King John asked one of his advisors, a gray-bearded old noble with a cane. "How can we stop the fighting?"

"One king, one country!" the advisor declared, stomping his cane on the ground. "Just as they do in France and Spain! One king, one country, one religion! We must choose one religion for Transylvania. Everyone will follow it, and then we will have no more fighting."

King John didn't think that would work, but something obviously had to be done. Talking was better than arguing, and so, as his mother and Dr. Biandrata had suggested, King John invited preachers from different religions to come to his court and talk about religion, and they came. Dr. Biandrata invited his friend Francis Dávid (*pronounced DA-veed*), and he came. The preachers talked . . . and talked and talked and talked. Sometimes, they gave up talking to argue with each other, and sometimes they argued so much that King John was afraid they would give up arguing to start fighting, maybe even with swords!

But the talks went on, day after day, and no one was hurt. One man talked very well, and he convinced people in every discussion that he had. That man was Francis Dávid, Dr. Biandrata's friend. Nowadays, we would call Francis Dávid's religion Unitarianism, because he said that God was one being instead of three. He said God was a Unity, not a Trinity. King John decided he liked Francis Dávid, and he liked the religion, too. He decided to become a Unitarian, and in the year 1569, he did.

"One king, one country, one religion!" the old noble had said, but, "We need not think alike to love alike," Francis Dávid said, and King John agreed. He wanted to be a good and wise ruler over all of the people in the land. At a meeting in the town of Torda, he issued the Edict of Torda, a special law. The law said that "no one shall be reviled for their religion by anyone," and he allowed the people of Transylvania to choose the religion they thought was best for them.

On the fourteenth of January, 1571, King John Sigismund, the first and only Unitarian king in history, declared that Unitarianism was one of the official religions of his realm in Transylvania, and that people could worship as they chose. And even today, in that place beyond the forests called Transylvania, which is now part of the country of Romania, there are Unitarian churches, the oldest Unitarian churches in the world. Unitarians have lived there for over four hundred years, and Unitarians live there still.

More About the Edict of Torda

BY 1547, SEVEN YEARS after the death of King John I, the country of Hungary had been formally divided into three parts: Transylvania and some of eastern Hungary for Isabella and young John, the northern and western parts for Ferdinand I of Austria, and a large central part for Sultan Suleyman I of the Ottoman Empire.

In 1557, in response to a request of the Transylvanian Diet meeting at the town of Torda, Queen Isabella issued an edict in her son's name. The edict proclaimed:

> Inasmuch as We and Our Most Serene Son have assented to the most instant supplication of the Peers of the Realm, that each person maintain whatever religious faith he wishes, with old or new rituals, while We at the same time leave it to their judgment to do as they please in the matter of faith, just so long, however, as they bring no harm to bear on anyone at all, least the followers of a new religion be a source of irritation to the old profession of faith or become in some way injurious to its followers—therefore, Peers of the Realm, for the sake of procuring the peace of the churches and of stilling the controversies that have arisen in the gospel teaching, we

have decreed to establish a national synod, wherein, in the presence of devoted ministers of the Word of God as well as of other men of rank, genuine comparisons of doctrine may be made and, under God's guidance, dissension and differences of opinion in religion may be removed.

Isabella died two years after the edict was issued, but the synods and discussions continued during her son's reign. In 1568, King John issued another Edict of Torda that confirmed and strengthened the edict of 1557. It's sometimes referred to as "The Edict of Religious Toleration." He and most of his court converted to Unitarianism in 1569. On January 14, 1571, John declared Unitarianism a "received" [official] religion of his realm, along with Catholicism, Lutheranism, and Calvinism. The next day, he was hurt in a carriage accident. He died from his injuries a few months later, at age thirty-one.

After John's death, Unitarianism was sometimes tolerated, sometimes persecuted. Francis Dávid was convicted of heretical innovations to the Unitarian religion and died in the dungeon at Deva. Today, there are eighty thousand Unitarians in Romania.

∽

1770

The Wind of Change

Over two hundred years ago (when the United States of America was still the thirteen colonies), there lived a man named John Murray. John Murray and his wife, Eliza, lived in the country of England. They were very religious people. Every Sunday they got up early, got dressed, ate their breakfast, and went to church. Sometimes, John Murray would preach a sermon and talk to the people about God.

Now, their church was not a place to be happy. No one smiled. No one laughed. No one sang. Because the followers of that religion, called Calvinism, believed that almost all of the people were going to hell. They believed that God would let only a few people into heaven. No matter what people did, even if they were really, really nice and tried really, really hard to be good, they still couldn't go to heaven. No matter what. And so the religion in that church was a very serious business, and the people were expected to be serious, too.

But one day, John and Eliza Murray heard of a man named Mr. Relly. Mr. Relly was of a different religion, a religion that said people didn't have to go to hell, a religion where people could be happy. Finally, after talking about it for weeks, John and Eliza decided to listen to what Mr. Relly had to say. The next Sunday, they got up early, got dressed, ate their breakfast, and they went to Mr. Relly's church instead of their own.

At that church, people smiled. Someone actually laughed. When it came time for the sermon, Mr. Relly got up to preach. He said, "God loves all his children. God doesn't have favorites. Everyone, everyone in the universe, has the chance to go to heaven and be saved from the fires of hell. Salvation is universal." Mr. Relly was a Universalist, and after hearing his sermon, John and Eliza decided they were Universalists, too.

But the people at their old church weren't Universalists. "Mr. Murray!" they said, very stern. "Have you and your wife been going to hear that heretic, Mr. Relly?"

"Yes, sirs, we have," answered John Murray.

"And do you believe such nonsense, that all people have the chance to be saved?"

"Yes, sirs, we do."

"Mr. Murray!" they said, appalled. "You mustn't say such things!"

"Yes," said John Murray, "I must."

And they said, "Oh, no, you won't!"

And he said, "Oh, yes, I will!"

And they said, "Well, you can't say them here! You and your wife both have to leave!"

Poor John and Eliza Murray! None of their old friends would talk to them, and they were lonely and sad. Then Eliza had a baby, which made them happy for a while, but then the baby got sick and Eliza got sick, and John had to borrow money to pay the doctors. He borrowed more and more money and went to more and more doctors, but they couldn't help. His wife and his baby died. And then he was arrested, because he couldn't pay back the money he had borrowed.

So there John Murray sat, all alone in a cell, with no job, no money, no family, and no friends. He decided he had failed God and failed his family and failed himself. He decided he was never going to be part of a church again. He decided he was never going to preach again.

Ever.

After a few days, Eliza's brother paid the money that John owed, and so John was set free. But John wasn't happy in England anymore. He wanted a new life in a new land. He bought a ticket on the sailing ship *Hand-in-Hand*. The ship had great white sails that were filled by the wind, and the wind blew and blew. The wind blew John Murray all the way across the Atlantic Ocean, far away from England and to a new land.

But the wind blew John Murray to a place he hadn't planned to go—he ended up in New Jersey, instead of New York. The *Hand-in-Hand* became stranded on a sandbar off the coast, and the sailors couldn't move the ship because the wind kept blowing them into shore. Because there wasn't much food on the ship, John Murray climbed out and waded ashore through a marsh. Near Barnegat Bay, he met a farmer named Thomas Potter, who invited him into his house and gave him supper.

Now, Thomas Potter also believed in a loving God, and he believed in Universal Salvation. He believed in it so much, that ten years before John Murray had shown up on his doorstep, blown in by that wind, Thomas Potter had built a little church all by himself. For ten years, he had been waiting and waiting for the right preacher to come.

And now the preacher was here! But John Murray didn't want to preach. Not at all. Thomas Potter argued with him and talked to him and prayed over him, and still John Murray didn't want to preach. "I swore I would never preach again," John Murray said. "Ever."

But Thomas Potter said, "I believe that the wind that brought you here to my door was the breath of God. I believe God sent you here to preach in the church I have built. I believe that the wind will never change until you have preached to the people a message from God. Tell me, sir, if that wind does not change by Sunday morning, will you take that as a sign from God himself that you should preach again?"

John Murray thought and thought about that, and finally he said, "I will."

The wind blew. The wind blew and blew for days, and it kept the boat from leaving the shore. The wind didn't change. So, on Sunday morning, on the thirtieth of September in the year 1770, while that wind was still blowing, John Murray got up early, got dressed, ate his breakfast, and went to church.

And he preached.

He preached in the church Thomas Potter had built, and he preached of a loving and caring God. He preached of Universal Salvation, the idea that all people everywhere in the universe could go to heaven and be saved. He said, "You possess only a small light, but uncover it, let it shine!"

And afterward, when the people came to him and thanked him for his sermon, John Murray changed. He changed his mind about joining a church again, and he changed his mind about being a preacher.

In 1779, in the town of Gloucester, Massachusetts, John Murray became the minister of the very first organized Universalist church in America. He traveled and preached in many places in the United States and became known as one of the founders of American Universalism.

The church that Thomas Potter built doesn't exist anymore. It was torn down years ago. But Universalists are still there—Unitarian Universalists now. If you go to New Jersey, there on the shores of Barnegat Bay, you can stay at a special Unitarian Universalist retreat center named Murray Grove, in honor of John Murray, the man who decided to preach again and to let his light shine.

More About John Murray

JOHN MURRAY IS FEATURED ON pages 61–68 of *The UU Kids Book* and in Session 9 of *We Believe*. The hymnal *Singing the Living Tradition* contains one reading by John Murray, No. 704.

John Murray is sometimes called the Father of American Universalism, but Universalism had emerged in central New England well before his arrival. Elhanan Winchester, Adams Streeter, Caleb Rich, and the Davis family were influential in the New England movement. John Murray and James Relly and their brand of Universalism came from Methodism. John and Eliza Murray were excommunicated from their Methodist church in 1760.

In 1774, four years after his sermon in Thomas Potter's church, Murray settled in Gloucester, Massachusetts, though he continued to travel about from place to place, preaching. In 1779, Murray and seventeen others of Gloucester split from the First Church of Christ Congregational and formed the Independent Church of Christ. They built a meetinghouse and held their first service on Christmas Day, 1780. Five years later, after being harassed both legally and physically by other denominations, Murray was instrumental in organizing the scattered congregations and choosing the name "Universalists." This helped the new faith gain legal recognition and protection and earned John Murray the title "Father of American Universalism."

In 1788, John Murray and Judith Sargent Stevens (her husband, John Stevens, had died the year before) were married. She became well known for her writings. In 1793, Murray settled in a parish ministry on Hanover Street in Boston. He remained there until his death in 1815.

Those Awful Unitarians

THE BALTIMORE SERMON

1819

Nearly two hundred years ago, when tall-masted ships sailed on the oceans and horses clip-clopped on cobble-stoned streets, two young ladies named Amelia and Emily were walking in the city of Baltimore. It was a warm spring day, and Amelia and Emily twirled their parasols on their shoulders and lifted the hems of their long skirts to step over the puddles of rain.

"Good day to you, ladies!" called a gentleman, and he tipped his hat to them and smiled.

Amelia smiled back and said, "Good day!"

But when the gentleman had gone by, Emily clutched at her friend's arm and said, "Amelia! Don't you know who that is?"

15

"No."

"That's Mr. Jared Sparks. He's going to be the minister of that new church with the big dome on Franklin Street."

Amelia gasped. "You don't mean . . ."

"Yes! Mr. Sparks . . . ," and Emily looked around, then lowered her voice before she said, "is a Unitarian."

"Oh, dear!" Amelia turned to look at the gentleman, who was just disappearing around a corner. "And he seemed like such a pleasant man."

Emily sniffed. "Father says those Unitarians are all nonbelievers."

Amelia said, "But I heard that Mr. Sparks is going to be ordained on Wednesday."

Emily sniffed again. "They may call it 'ordained,' but Father says he would never call a Unitarian minister 'Reverend,' because they're not proper Christians. They don't even believe that Jesus was the son of God!"

"Oh my goodness!" Amelia said. "Mama said one of their ministers, a Mr. William Ellery Channing, will be coming all the way down from Boston to give a sermon, and a great many other of their ministers will be in Baltimore, too."

This time Emily giggled. "No one will hear Mr. Channing's sermon, unless they're sitting in the very first pew. People say that in the grand new church those Unitarians built, it's simply impossible to hear, which is a very good thing."

"Yes, it is," Amelia agreed. "That sort of Unitarian nonsense shouldn't be spread around." And with that declaration, the two young ladies continued on their walk, stepping over puddles and twirling their parasols on their way.

William Ellery Channing did come to Baltimore, all the way down from Boston. Dozens of other Unitarian ministers came, too. They held a special ordination ceremony for Mr. Jared Sparks, and he became the Reverend Jared Sparks, the official minister of the church.

And the Reverend Channing (because Unitarians did call their ministers "reverend") did preach a sermon that day. It's true that in that new church with the big dome not very many people could hear the sermon, but over ten thousand people read it, because it was printed and sold all around the United States.

Now, back then, as Amelia and Emily knew, "Unitarian" wasn't considered a polite word. People preferred to be called "liberal Christians in a Congregationalist church." But the title of William Ellery Channing's sermon on that day in 1819 was "Unitarian Christianity."

"It is our name," he said. "We must not shrink from it."

Two years after Mr. Channing's sermon in Baltimore, over one hundred Congregationalist churches had declared themselves to be Unitarian. Six years after the sermon, a group of ministers created the American Unitarian Association. They were proud of that name.

And so are we.

More About the Baltimore Sermon

WILLIAM ELLERY CHANNING'S words appear in *Singing the Living Tradition* in readings No. 592, "The Free Mind," and No. 652, "The Great End in Religious Instruction."

Channing was born in Newport, Rhode Island, in 1780. In 1803, five years after graduating from Harvard University, he became the pastor of the Federal Street Congregational Church in Boston. (The church constructed a new building on Arlington Street in 1861. It is now the Arlington Street Unitarian Universalist Church.) His historic sermon in Baltimore on May 5, 1819, spelled out the differences between the two sects within the Congregationalist faith: the Trinitarian sect (belief in the triune deity of Father, Son, and Holy Ghost) and the Unitarian sect (belief in one God only). Many churches in New England split over this issue. In May of 1825, six years after his sermon, the American Unitarian Association was formed.

Channing encouraged the use of music in worship services and helped organize the Unitarian Sunday School Society in 1827. He was influential in the Transcendentalist literary movement and remained pastor at the Federal Street Church until his death in 1842.

The church on Franklin Street was designed by the French architect Maximilien Godefroy. Eventually, a ceiling was constructed across the bottom of the dome to keep the sound from being lost in the fifty-five-foot high curve. The church is the oldest building in the United States that was designed for and has been continuously used by Unitarians.

Jared Sparks was born in Connecticut in 1789 and graduated from Harvard Divinity School in 1818. He was the minister at the First Independent Church in Baltimore from 1819 to 1823. He was also chaplain of the U.S. House of Representatives from 1821 to 1823. He moved to Boston and from 1824 to 1830 he was the owner and editor of the *North American Review.* A historian, he wrote biographies of George Washington and Benjamin Franklin. Sparks taught history at Harvard University from 1838 to 1849, then served as the university's president for the next four years. He died in Cambridge, Massachusetts, in 1866.

A Plain and Simple Beauty

n the city of Prague, in the land of Czechoslovakia, in the year nineteen hundred and twenty-three, a time between the two World Wars, there was a church. But the building did not look much like a church. Some churches have towers with bells that ring out over the land. Some churches have tall spires that reach to the sky. Some churches have massive doors of carved wood, or enormous windows of stained glass with colored light shining through. Some churches have great organs with hundreds of pipes, from small ones like drinking straws to huge ones that touch the ceiling. Some churches have statues or pictures or candles or chalices.

This church had none of those things. It had no bells, no spires, no stained glass windows. It had no organ to make beautiful music. It didn't even have a piano. It had no carvings of wood or statues of stone. It had no candles or chalices. It had no flowers.

The church did have some things. It had four walls and a ceiling and a floor. It had a door and a few windows. It had some hard wooden chairs. But that was all, plain and simple.

Except . . . the church also had people who came to it every Sunday, and they were the most important part of the church of all. Because without people, a church—any church—is just a building, no matter how tall its spires, or how loud its bells.

"We have a plain and simple church," the people declared, "because we are plain and simple people. We need nothing more."

The church also had one other very important thing. It had a minister, and his name was Norbert Čapek (*pronounced CHAH-peck*). He had been the minister at the plain and simple church for two years. Every Sunday, Minister Čapek went to church, and he spoke to the people while they listened, sitting quiet and still in those hard wooden chairs. When he was done speaking, the people talked a little bit among themselves, and then they went home. And that was all—no music, no candles, no food. Not even coffee or doughnuts.

Minister Čapek had wondered, sometimes, if there might be something—perhaps just a little bit of something—more. He wrote some songs, and the people sang them, but nothing else came to his mind, so the church went on, as plain and simple as before.

Springtime came to the city of Prague, in the land of Czechoslovakia, in the year nineteen hundred and twenty-three, and Norbert Čapek went for a stroll. The rains had come, the birds were singing, and flowers were blooming all over the land. The world was beautiful.

Then an idea came to him, simple and clear, plain as the day. The next Sunday, he asked all the people of the church to bring a flower or a budding branch, or even a twig. Each person was to bring one.

"What kind?" they asked. "What color? What size?"

"You choose," he said. "Each of you choose what you like."

And so, on the next Sunday, which was the first day of summer, the people came with flowers of all different colors and sizes and kinds. There were yellow daisies and red roses. There were white lilies and blue asters, dark-eyed pansies and light green leaves. Pink and purple, orange and gold—there were all those colors and more. Flowers filled all the vases, and the church wasn't so plain and simple anymore.

Minister Čapek spoke to the people while they listened, sitting quiet and still in those hard wooden chairs. "These flowers are like ourselves," he said. "Different colors, different shapes, and different sizes, each needing different kinds of care—but each beautiful, each important and special, in its own way."

When he was done speaking, the people talked a little bit among themselves, and then they each chose a different flower from the vases before they went home. And that was all—and it was beautiful, plain and simple as the day.

More About the Flower Communion

NORBERT ČAPEK IS FEATURED IN Sessions 28 and 29 of *Around the Church, Around the Year*. The hymnal *Singing the Living Tradition* contains three of his hymns (No. 8 "Mother Spirit, Father Spirit"; No. 28, "View the Starry Realm"; and No. 78, "Color and Fragrance") and two readings (No. 723, "The Flower Communion Prayer," and No. 724, "Consecration of the Flowers").

Čapek was born in 1870 in Bohemia, which was part of the Austro-Hungarian Empire. He was raised in the Roman Catholic faith but converted to the Baptist faith at the age of eighteen. He became a minister and a missionary and was very active in that religion. As World War I began, he feared arrest by the Austrian authorities for his nationalistic and anti-Catholic writings, so he moved to the United States in 1914. He continued his ministerial work in the Baptist churches, but in 1919 he resigned, having decided that he could no longer in good conscience be a Baptist.

In 1921, he and his wife, Maja, and their children joined the First Unitarian Church of Essex County in New Jersey. Six months later, the Čapek family left for their native land of Bohemia, which had become a part of Czechoslovakia after the war. There they started a Unitarian church, with Norbert and, after 1926, Maja as ordained ministers. Twenty years later, it was the largest Unitarian church in the world, with over thirty-two hundred members.

However, war came once again. Norbert was arrested by the Gestapo in 1941, spent a year in prison, then was sent to the concentration camp at Dachau. He died in 1942 at Hartheim Castle in Austria, poisoned by gas. Maja had gone to the United States in 1939 to help raise funds for the refugee program that was sponsored by the Unitarians and the Friends (Quakers). She stayed in the United States for the duration of the war, serving as a Unitarian minister in New Bedford, Massachusetts, then working to help refugees. She learned of her husband's death after the war was over. She died in 1966.

Circles
of Light

n the dark nights and darker days of World War II, when guns blazed all over Europe and airplanes dropped death from the sky, some Unitarians in the United States decided to help the refugees, the people who were trying to escape from the war. So, the Unitarian Service Committee was formed. The committee members went to Europe to try to bring the refugees safely out of the war.

But some of those refugees spoke German, some spoke French, some spoke Italian or Yiddish or some other language. Dr. Charles Joy, who was in charge of the committee, knew that the Unitarians needed a symbol that everyone could recognize, no matter what language they spoke or what country they were from.

In 1941, in the city of Lisbon, Dr. Joy asked the artist Hans Deutsch for help. Hans Deutsch was a refugee himself. In fact, he'd been a refugee more than once. He had been born in Austria, but when the Nazis invaded his country, he fled to Paris. Then, the Nazis invaded Paris! So, Hans Deutsch fled to Portugal, where he met Dr. Joy.

"Draw us a symbol," Dr. Joy asked. "Make it look important and official, so it will impress the officials of different countries, yet have it show the spirit of our work, which is to help and to serve."

And so, with pencil and with ink, Hans Deutsch drew a chalice with a flame, surrounded by a circle of protection and love. Refugees all over Europe came to know and trust that sign, and the flaming chalice became a symbol of freedom and hope during the dark nights and darker days of that war.

Over thirty years later, in 1976, after the Unitarians and the Universalists had joined to form the Unitarian Universalist Association, that one circle drawn around the flaming chalice became two. (That's the symbol on the hymnbooks.) One circle is for Unitarians; one circle is for Universalists. The circles aren't one inside the other; they're intertwined. They're connected, just as all of us are connected to each other and to everything in the world.

The chalice isn't in the middle of the circles; it's a little off to one side, to leave space for other ideas and other ways. There's always room for more in Unitarian Universalism.

That picture of the chalice in the double circle has been used officially since 1976. Real flaming chalices have been used in some of our churches for over fifty years. In

1981, the Reverend David Poul lit a chalice at a General Assembly meeting during the Service of the Living Tradition, which is held to celebrate the lives of UU ministers. Many of the ministers who were there that day went home to their churches and fellowships, and they decided to get chalices of their own.

Today, all over the world, Unitarian Universalists light the Flaming Chalice. We light one every Sunday when we gather for worship. Some of us have a smaller chalice in our houses, and we light a chalice before every meal, or at other special times.

We have all kinds of chalices. Chalices are carved out of wood, shaped out of glass, or molded out of clay. We even wear them as jewelry or as pictures on our clothes. Chalices come in lots of different shapes and sizes and colors, just like Unitarian Universalists.

The Flaming Chalice was drawn more than sixty years ago, and it is still a symbol of freedom, and hope, and light. It's a symbol of learning and caring and love. It's our symbol, the symbol of Unitarian Universalism.

More About the Flaming Chalice

THE FLAMING CHALICE IS FEATURED in Story 2 in *Around the Church, Around the Year,* and on pages 44–45 and 89 of *The UU Kids Book.*

Unitarian Universalism is neither the first nor the only religion to use a chalice or a flame as a sacred symbol. Throughout history, drinking vessels have been used on altars all over the world, with offerings such as water, milk, clarified butter, blood, or wine. Dr. Joy noted that the chalice Hans Deutsch had drawn was "the kind of chalice which the Greeks and Romans put on their altars." Jesus shared a cup with his disciples, and many Christian denominations continue this tradition today. The cauldron of Ceirdwyn offers rebirth, and the Holy Grail continues to inspire new stories. A chalice symbolizes community, life-giving nourishment, and love.

Fire is perhaps the most ancient of sacred symbols, from the time when our ancestors first gathered around a hearth at night and looked to the sun at day. People light lamps and candles in cathedrals, temples, mosques, and houses of worship. Bonfires celebrate great events, and eternal flames guard our tombs. As matter becomes energy, the dancing flame both illuminates and destroys. Fire signifies knowledge, with its vast potential for creation, transformation, and destruction, all at the same time.

Yet when the flame rises from the chalice, that fire of knowledge is bound by that circle of community and love. The flame burns steadily; it does not rage out of control. The light illuminates; it does not blind. So also does Unitarian Universalism provide a steadfast illumination in our lives, and yet it does not eclipse other flames. Hans Deutsch wrote, "I am not what you may actually call a believer. But if your kind of life is the profession of your faith—as it is, I feel sure—then religion, ceasing to be magic and mysticism, becomes confession to practical philosophy and—what is more—to active, really useful social work. And this religion . . . is one to which even a 'godless' fellow like myself can say wholeheartedly, 'Yes!'"

nitarian Universalist. That's the name we say when someone asks us, "What religion are you?" And then they usually say, "A Uni-what?"

"Unitarian Universalist," we say again, but often, the name by itself doesn't seem to explain very much.

Perhaps that's because "Unitarian Universalist" is not really "a name by itself." It's two names together, because we come from two religions: the Unitarians and the Universalists.

Both religions have roots far back in the Protestant Reformation, nearly four hundred years ago. Both religions were established in the United States around the time of the American Revolution, over two hun-

Merging Streams

dred years ago. Both religions had much in common. They both believed in the importance of social justice, religious education, and tolerance of different beliefs. In the 1800s, the Reverend Thomas Starr King (who was raised as a Universalist and became a Unitarian minister, and so perhaps might be described as a Universalist Unitarian) said that the only reason that Unitarians and Universalists hadn't already joined together was that they were too closely related to be married.

And yet, they did "marry." Not that it was easy. The courtship took years, and not everyone was interested. Some people said, "Why not?" but other people said, "Why? What will we have to change? What will be different? What will we lose? What will we gain?"

They weren't quite sure. So, they formed committees and commissions to find out. There were studies and papers. There were meetings and panels and polls. People talked and talked and talked. (These were Unitarians and Universalists, after all.)

Finally, in 1959, nearly one hundred years after the idea had first been proposed, most people were convinced it would be a good thing to join together. They were saying "Why not?" instead of "Why?" So they agreed on a "Plan to Consolidate," and they printed the plan in a little blue book. One thousand delegates (six hundred Unitarians, four hundred Universalists) gathered in Syracuse, New York, to vote on the plan, but before they voted, they talked some more.

They talked about what to name the new religion. Should it be Universalist Unitarian or Unitarian Universalist? Should there be a hyphen between the two names? Or should they choose a totally new name?

They talked about making fifty-seven different changes to the "Plan to Consolidate," and each group—the Unitarians and the Universalists—had to vote on each and every single one. It took them days.

But they did it! The delegates agreed on the plan to consolidate and become the Unitarian Universalist Association.

Then it was up to the churches to decide whether or not to agree. Now, usually, when the associations held a plebiscite—votes from all the people in each church, instead of one vote from that church's delegate—only about 20 percent or so of the churches would even bother to reply. But this time, in order for the consolidation to succeed, 75 percent of the churches had to vote, and 75 percent of those churches had to say, "Yes, we want to join."

"It'll never happen," said some people. "You'll never get that many people to vote, let alone vote yes."

But the delegates had worked too hard and too long on the "Plan to Consolidate" to let the vote die. So they called each church, and they asked members to vote. "Vote 'yes' or vote 'no,' whichever you choose, but vote!"

And they did. But not 20 percent. Not 50 percent. Not 75. More. Over 90 percent of the churches voted on that plan, and nearly 90 percent of them voted "Yes." In May of 1961, the American Unitarian Association and the Universalist Church of America consolidated with each other, and the Unitarian Universalist Association was officially formed.

And so here we are, more than forty years later, with two names and one religion: Unitarian Universalist.

More About Consolidation

DETAILS ON THE CONSOLIDATION may be found in *The Premise and the Promise: The Story of the Unitarian Universalist Association* by Warren R. Ross. *Unitarian Universalist Origins: Our Historic Faith*, a UUA pamphlet by Mark W. Harris is a useful resource as well.

Unitarianism takes its name from the belief in the unity of God—the idea that God is one being, not a trinity of Father, Son, and Holy Spirit. Universalism takes its name from its belief in universal salvation—the idea that everyone in the universe will eventually be saved from hell and go to heaven. Both ideas existed among the early Christians; both ideas were condemned as heresy after the Nicene Council of 325. After that, people professing belief in either Unitarianism or Universalism were persecuted, sometimes even killed.

As the Protestant Reformation moved across Europe in the 1500s, both Unitarian and Universalist ideas resurfaced more strongly, and the ideas went with the European immigrants to North America. In 1770 a Universalist church was established in Gloucester, Massachusetts. The denomination was organized in 1793. Unitarian churches were an outgrowth of the Congregationalist tradition of the Puritans, and the American Unitarian Association was organized in Boston, Massachusetts, in 1825. Both religions flourished in the 1800s, with many members advocating the abolition of slavery, women's rights, humane treatment of prisoners and those in asylums, better education and health care, and other social reforms.

Unitarians and Universalists had often worked together in these efforts, and by the 1950s, many had decided it was time to make the partnership official. The "Plan to Consolidate" was written, discussed, amended, voted upon, and adopted in 1959. A plebiscite was held, and the great majority of the members of the churches voted yes. In 1960, 887 Universalist delegates and 430 Unitarian delegates gathered in Boston to ratify the outcome of the plebiscite and to formally establish the Unitarian Universalist Association. The final vote was more than five to one in favor.

Hundreds of ministers joined the delegates for a celebratory worship service, and all joined in singing,

> As tranquil streams that meet and merge
> And flow as one to seek the sea,
> Our kindred fellowships unite
> To build a church that shall be free.
> (Hymn 145 in *Singing the Living Tradition*)

Donald Harrington delivered the sermon "Unitarian Universalism: Yesterday, Today, and Tomorrow," and at the end of the service, the delegates promised, "We declare our allegiance to the new Unitarian Universalist Association, and pledge our lives, our fortunes, and our faith to its highest purposes and sure upbuilding."

The Long, Slow Swell of the Sea

I speak now of a time of great changes, of the ebb and the flow of an ever-advancing tide, and of a long, slow swell of the sea.

The women were rising.

The women had always been there, of course, from the beginning. Across the globe, down through the ages, in the homes of their families, the women fetched the water, gathered and prepared the food, made the clothes, tended the fires, and cared for the children, the sick, and the old. In this country, through the centuries, in the sacred places of their communities, the women cleaned the buildings, decorated the altars, brought the food, sang in the choir, helped the poor and the needy, and listened from the pews. From the beginning, the women had been there.

But mostly, they had been silent, and mostly, they had held no power in their hands. Mostly, the decisions had been made by the men.

No more. The women were rising, with the long, slow swell of the sea.

In the year 1977, a group of women gathered around a butcher block in the kitchen of the Unitarian Universalist Church in Lexington, Massachusetts. They decided that the women should be—and would be—heard. That summer, the Unitarian Universalist General Assembly agreed to their proposal, and the "Women and Religion Resolution" was formed. Our bylaws were updated, our songs were revised, our principles reframed—so that the word "he" became "he and she" and "man" became "people." A seventh principle was added—respect for the interdependent web of all life, man and woman, female and male, and stones and butterflies and trees. The words weren't the only things to change; people's ideas were changing, too.

The women were rising, and the tide was flowing over the land.

In 1980, a great gathering was held, a "Convocation on Feminist Theology," and people came from all over the land. To honor their journeys, journeys through space and time, journeys with joy and pain, journeys completed, journeys ongoing, and also journeys not yet begun, two women, Lucile Longview and Carolyn McDade, created a ceremony of water-sharing for them all.

For the women were rising, and water had carried them there.

From the mouth of the Mississippi River, from the Atlantic and Pacific . . . the women and the waters came. From the mountains and the deserts, from rivers and streams, from drops of rain . . . the women and the waters came. From the oceans of the ages, from the ancient womb of life that created us all . . . the women and the waters came.

In a circle of hundreds they gathered. In a circle of hundreds they sang. In a circle unbroken they listened to each other's stories, and they listened to the waters as they fell. For the women came forth with their water, those waters from all over the land, and they mingled the waters in a great earthen bowl.

Then, as each had given to the waters, each took from the waters. In this taking, they reclaimed the water. In this taking, they reclaimed the Earth. They reclaimed their history. They laid claim to their future, and the future of all living things. A vow and a promise, to each other and to themselves.

Then in their circle of hundreds they sang "We're coming home."

For the women were rising, and the waters were rising, and great changes were sweeping over the land, with the long, slow swell of the sea.

And the women—and the men—were all coming home.

More About the Water Ritual

THE SONG "COMING HOME" was composed by Carolyn McDade for the Water Ritual. The hymnal *Singing the Living Tradition* contains three songs by her: No. 121, "We'll Build a Land"; No. 123, "Spirit of Life"; and No. 346, "Come, Sing a Song With Me."

Lucile Schuck Longview and Carolyn McDade created the Water Ritual worship service for the "Women and Religion Convocation on Feminist Theology," which was held in East Lansing, Michigan, in November of 1980. In attendance were approximately 350 women and a few men. Eight women brought water:

- Linda Pinti (from a nearby stream in East Lansing)
- Marinell Hartogensis (from the desert near Albuquerque)
- Edith Fletcher (from a mountain lake in New York State)
- Jean Bramadet (from the Assiniboine River in Winnipeg)
- Jean Zoerheide (rainwater from Maryland)
- Vivian Guild (from the mouth of the Mississippi)
- Rosemary Matson (from the Pacific Ocean near Carmel by the Sea)
- Pat Simon (from the Atlantic Ocean)

Since that time, the Water Communion has become a common ingathering ceremony at many UU congregations, usually taking place after the summer holidays as people bring back waters from their travels.

The Women and Religion Resolution was passed by the UUA General Assembly in June of 1977, in response to the movement spearheaded by Lucile S. Longview. She believed that "of the major obstacles to equality shared by women everywhere, religions and the attitudes, prejudices and assumptions which they perpetuate, stand high on the list," and she set out to eliminate those obstacles in the UUA. The group that gathered in the church kitchen in January 1977 included Lucile, Jan Bjorklund, Billie and David Drew, Edith Fletcher, Nancy Greenleaf, Tina Jas, and Jean Zoerheide. Their resolution was modified and strengthened by the Joseph Priestley District, then affirmed by the UU Women's Federation before being presented to the General Assembly. It passed unanimously.

In 1978, UUA president Paul Carnes appointed the Reverend Leslie (Cronin) Westbrook to be the Minister to Women and Religion. An eight-member Continental Women and Religion Committee was appointed to work with her and to report directly to him. The committee and the Reverend Leslie Westbrook worked with the UUA staff in Education, Ministry, and Extension to develop material, programs, and policies to implement the intent of the resolution. The process was sometimes slow, but in 1985 the principles were reframed, and in 1993 the new hymnbook, *Singing the Living Tradition*, was created with language that includes both women and men.

However, the changes from the Women and Religion Resolution go deeper than words. Throughout our history, women in the Unitarian and the Universalist ministries had been few and far between, as this timeline shows.

1853 Antoinette Brown is the first woman to be ordained by a Congregationalist church in New York. She eventually leaves it and becomes a Unitarian.

1860 Lydia Ann Jenkins is the first woman to be ordained by the Universalists.

1863 Olympia Brown is ordained by Universalists. 1868 Phebe Hanaford is ordained by Universalists in New England.

1871 Celia Burleigh is the first woman ordained as a Unitarian minister.

1880 Mary Safford (a leader of the Iowa Sisterhood) is ordained by the Unitarians. (Other sisters include Eleanor Gordon, Marion Murdock, Caroline Bartlett Crane, Eliza Tupper Wilkes, Florence Buck, Mary Colson, Mary Leggett, Adele Fuchs, Mary Jenney Howe, Ida Hultin, Rowena Mann, Celia Parker Woolley, and others.)

1892 According to the United States. census and the Women's Ministerial Conference, there are thirty-two ordained Universalist women ministers and sixteen ordained Unitarian women ministers.

1893 Unitarians have nineteen women ministers. Universalists have thirty-six (twenty-seven ordained, nine licensed to preach).

1906 Rowena Morse Mann is made a minister, the last of the Iowa Sisterhood to be ordained. She retires early because she can find no available pulpit.

1914 According to Florence Kollock Crooker (a Universalist minister married to a Unitarian), out of the 640 Universalist ministers listed in the yearbook, 75 (8.5 percent) are women.

1917 Clara Cook Helvie is ordained at Unitarian church in Wheeling, West Virginia, the first Unitarian woman ordained since 1906.

1920 The women's suffrage amendment passes. Universalists have ordained eighty-eight women; Unitarians have ordained forty-two.

1935 Roger Etz, Universalist general superintendent, writes that there is "tremendous prejudice against women" and that it is "practically impossible" to find them jobs. In the three decades between 1920 and 1950, only one Unitarian woman and nine Universalist women are ordained.

1950 Maryell Cleary ordained. She does not settle in a ministry until 1971.

1959 Sophia Lyon Fahs is ordained a Unitarian minister at the age of eighty-two at Bethesda, Maryland, church.

1960 There are no settled parish Unitarian women ministers, and only three Universalist.

1961 Unitarians and Universalists consolidate to form the UUA.

In the two and a half decades since the Women and Religion Resolution was passed in 1977, the number of women ministers increased sharply. Other cultural factors contributed to this, but the UUA's active encouragement played a large role. At first, the majority of women ministers were involved in specialty work or in religious education. By 1998, women were 45 percent of parish ministers, 85 percent of ministers of religious education, 62 percent of community ministers, 66 percent of field staff, and 47 percent of other UUA ministerial staff.

In March of 1999, the majority of the 853 actively engaged UU ministers were women (431 women and 422 men). The Women and Religion Resolution has challenged us as a denomination to examine our assumptions, our prejudices, and our most basic ideas. It has changed—and is changing—our world.

Who We Are

Seven Stories of UU Heroes

HOSEA BALLOU

(1771–1852)

O ver two hundred years ago, in a small house in a small town, on the edge of a forest of very big trees in the state of New Hampshire, there lived a small boy. His name was Hosea Ballou.

Hosea, just like other children, liked to learn and to do new things. He was always asking questions, about what and why and how. And, just like other children, Hosea liked to play. He liked to play hide-and-seek with his nine older brothers and sisters. He liked to play word games inside when it was rainy, and he liked to play tag outside when it was sunny. In the winter, he liked to jump into snowdrifts. In the summer, he liked to jump into the creek. In the fall, he liked to

Muddy Children

jump into leaf piles. And in the spring—why, spring was Hosea's favorite season of all—because in the spring, it would rain and rain and rain, and then Hosea could jump into mud.

Hosea, just like other children, loved mud. He liked it when it was soft and squishy, and he liked it when it was thick and sticky. If it didn't rain quite enough, that wasn't a problem. Hosea would carry the water to the dirt and create glorious mud puddles all of his own. He liked to poke sticks into puddles and see how deep the mud was. He liked to make mud pies and to build mud dams. He liked to jump in puddles hard with both feet and make the muddy water splash really high, so that the mud splattered all over his brothers' and sisters' clothes, and he loved to step in puddles v-e-r-y slowly, so that the mud oozed up just a little bit at a time between his toes.

Yes, Hosea loved mud.

Now, you can imagine that not everybody in his family liked mud quite as much as Hosea did. His mother had died when he was not quite two, so his older sisters took care of him. His sister who did laundry and scrubbed the family's dirty clothes in big washtubs didn't like having to scrub all that mud off Hosea's clothes—or off everybody else's clothes, either, after Hosea had stomped in a mud puddle extra hard.

His other older sister who kept the little children clean didn't like having to scrub all that mud off Hosea. And Hosea (just like other children) didn't like having baths, either, especially when it meant he had to stand in a washtub in front of the fire and have water dumped over his head. But his sisters loved him, so they took him home and washed him and dried him and made him clean.

Then Hosea's sisters went to their father and said, "Father, please tell Hosea to stop playing in the mud."

"Hosea," said his father, very sternly, "you should not play in the mud."

"Why?" asked Hosea, because (just like other children) asking questions was another thing he loved to do.

"Because," said his father, who was one of the preachers in the Baptist church the family went to, "just as we try to live a good life, to be kind to other people and to follow God's plan, we try to stay clean."

"Yes, Father," Hosea said, and after that day, he did indeed try to stay clean.

But it wasn't easy. He stopped stomping in the mud puddles on purpose and splashing muddy water everywhere, and he stopped making enormous mud pies, but sometimes the mud was just there. Then he had to walk through the mud to get across the yard to gather the eggs from the chickens. He had to walk in the mud to feed the pigs. And sometimes, when he was already muddy from doing his chores, he played in the mud, just a little bit, and got even muddier. His sisters, who loved him, took him home and washed him and dried him and made him all clean.

But Hosea's sisters went to their father again and said, "Father, please tell Hosea to stop playing in the mud."

"Hosea," said his father even more sternly, "you must not play in the mud."

"Yes, Father," Hosea said. He was sad, because he had truly tried not to get muddy, most of the time anyway. "Are you very angry with me, Father?"

"I am disappointed in you, Hosea, and I am a little angry with you."

Hosea hung his head and kicked at the dirt with his toes, then he dared to look up, just a little, to ask, "Do you still love me?"

"Hosea," said his father, and his father didn't sound stern anymore. "I will always love you, Hosea, no matter what you do."

"Even if I get muddy again?"

"Yes."

"Even if I get really, really muddy?"

"Yes."

"Even if I get mud all the way up to my eyebrows and between my fingers and my toes and in my hair?"

"Even then," his father said with a smile. Then he added, very stern again, "But remember, Hosea. You must try to stay clean."

"I'll remember, and I'll try," Hosea promised, and he did. He stayed clean, most of the time anyway. As he grew up, he stopped liking mud quite so much, but he still liked to ask questions about what and how and why.

"Father," Hosea asked when he was a teenager, "how can it be that our church believes that God will let only one in a thousand people into heaven, even if many of those thousand people lead good lives?" His father didn't have an answer for that question.

"Father," Hosea asked, "if I had the power to create a living creature, and if I knew that the creature would have a miserable life, would suffer and die and then go to hell and be miserable forever, and I went ahead and created it anyway, would that be a good thing or a bad thing? And would I be good or bad?"

His father didn't have an answer for that question, either. Hosea had to find his own answers. So he read the Bible, a book with many stories about religious people and about God. He went to some Universalist churches and asked more questions there. At the age of nineteen, Hosea decided that he believed in universal salvation, which is the idea that everyone everywhere—everyone in the universe—will be given salvation. Eventually, everyone will be "saved" from hell. And not only did Hosea believe that God would let more than one in a thousand people into heaven, Hosea Ballou believed God would eventually let everyone into heaven, good and bad.

"How can you believe that?" asked his father. "How can you believe that God would let bad people into heaven?"

"Because, Father, I remember what you told me when I was small. I believe that even if God is disappointed in his children or a little angry with them, he will always love them and want them to be happy, no matter what they do, and no matter how muddy they are."

More About Hosea Ballou

THE HYMNAL *Singing the Living Tradition* contains words from Hosea Ballou in No. 705, "If We Agree in Love."

Hosea Ballou was born in 1771, in the town of Richmond, New Hampshire, near the Massachusetts border. At that time, Richmond was a frontier settlement. Hosea was the tenth child of Maturin and Lydia Ballou. Maturin was a Baptist preacher, and Lydia died when Hosea was twenty months old. The family was poor, and except for a few months in 1790 and 1791, Hosea never attended school.

To his family's concern, Hosea converted to Universalism in his teens, joining a growing number of New Englanders who were moving away from their Calvinist roots. This movement was independent of the Universalism brought over from England by John Murray two decades before. When Ballou was nineteen, he began to preach, traveling from church to church in Vermont and Massachusetts as well as his native New Hampshire. In 1817, a new church was created for him in Boston so that he could preach Universalism regularly in that city. By the time Ballou died in 1852, Universalism had grown to half a million members, the sixth largest denomination in the United States at that time.

As far as I know, there is no historical evidence that Hosea liked mud more than any other child. The idea for this story came from Ballou's address at the Universalist General Convention, held in Boston in 1851. He summed up his belief in a God who, as a Father, loves all his children: "Your child has fallen into the mire, and its body and its garments are defiled. You cleanse it, and array it in clean robes. The query is, Do you love your child because you have washed it? Or, Did you wash it because you loved it?"

〜

(1810–1860)

The Turtle and the Voice of God

Once upon a time, nearly two hundred years ago, there lived a boy named Theodore Parker. He lived on a farm in the state of Massachusetts with his mother and his father and his ten older brothers and sisters. In the summer of 1814, when Theodore was almost—but not quite—four years old, he was finally old enough to go with his father for walks around their farm.

Theodore walked proudly next to his father, taking extra long strides to keep up. They walked by the chicken coop where the black-and-white speckled hens scratched all day in the dirt with their strong toes, and the rooster would cry "Cock-a-doodle-doo!" when he saw Theodore and his father go by.

They walked by the barn where the cows lived, and the calves would stop eating to stare at them with big brown eyes.

They walked by the pond where the dragonflies darted, and the frogs would leap ker-plunk, ker-splash into the water.

They walked by the fields where the corn grew tall, and the wind fluttered the tassels of corn silk way up high.

They walked by the pasture where the sheep grazed, and the ewes would call out "Baa-baa" as Theodore and his father went by.

They walked all the way around the farm every day, with Theodore walking a little farther and a little faster every day.

Now, one day, Theodore's father stopped to look at one of the sheep, and he kept looking for a very long time. Theodore was bored. So, Theodore put stones into little piles, but when he was done, his father was still looking at the sheep.

Then Theodore was very bored, so he climbed on a rock and jumped off it, and he did it over and over again, but when he was done, his father was still looking at that sheep.

So now Theodore was very, very bored. He picked up a stick and drew lines in the dirt, but when he was done, his father was looking at a different sheep.

"Father," Theodore asked, "may I please go home?"

His father looked at him, and looked at him some more. Theodore tried to stand up really tall, because he was almost—even if not quite—four years old. "It's a long way back to the house," his father told him.

"I won't get tired," Theodore promised.

"It's a crooked path in some places," his father warned.

"I know the way," Theodore said, standing up even taller.

"Well then," his father replied, smiling a little, "off you go."

So, Theodore went walking, with his stick in his hand. He walked by the pasture where the sheep were grazing, and the lambs called out "Baa-baa" as Theodore went by.

He walked by the fields where the corn grew tall, and the wind fluttered the tassels of corn silk way up high.

He walked by the pond where the dragonflies darted, and the frogs went leaping ker-plunk, ker-splash into the water. But then Theodore stopped and turned around and went back. He had seen something different today.

There, on a rock on the edge of the pond, lay a little striped turtle, enjoying the sunshine and the fine summer day. Theodore crept closer and closer, with his stick lifted high in his hand. He had seen other boys hit animals: squirrels and lizards and birds. Theodore had always been too little or too slow to hit anything, but this turtle was too slow to get away. Theodore lifted the stick as high as he could, and he started to swing.

"It is wrong!" boomed a voice, strong and clear, and Theodore stopped, frozen, with his stick still up in the air.

"Wrong!" said the voice one more time. Theodore looked all around. It wasn't his father's voice. It wasn't his mother's. It wasn't any of his ten older brothers or sisters. It wasn't the voice of a neighbor or even a friend. There was absolutely no one else around.

Theodore dropped the stick. The turtle crawled into the pool with a ker-sploosh and a ripple, and Theodore started to run.

He ran past the barn where the cows lived, and all the calves stopped eating and stared at him with big brown eyes.

He ran past the chicken coop where the rooster crowed every morning, and all the black-and-white speckled hens stopped scratching in the dirt to watch as he ran by.

He ran all the way home, and he ran straight into his mother's arms. He told her about the sheep and the stick and the turtle, and then he told her about the Voice. "Who was that?" Theodore wanted to know.

"Some call it your conscience," his mother told him. "But I call it the Voice of God. It guides us through our lives and tells us right from wrong. If you listen and obey it, then it will speak clearer and clearer, like the tolling of a bell, no matter how old you are."

"Even when I'm four?" Theodore asked.

His mother smiled. "Even when you're four."

"Even when I'm five?"

"Yes, even when you're five or six, and even up to fifty and sixty and beyond. But if you stop listening or don't obey it, then the Voice will get quieter and quieter, until you can't hear it at all."

⤳

Theodore grew up, and he got to be four, and he got to be five and six and seven and more, and he always listened to that Voice, every single day. When he was all grown up, he became a Unitarian minister.

People called him the "Yankee Crusader," because he was an abolitionist. He wanted to abolish slavery and help free the slaves. Some people agreed with him about slavery being wrong, but some people didn't. They argued with him and got angry with him, and some people even threatened to kill him.

But Theodore always did what he knew to be right, even when he was scared, because no matter how old he was, he always listened to that inner Voice of God.

More About Theodore Parker

THIS STORY IS BASED ON Theodore Parker's *Recollections of Boyhood*. It also appears in a different format in Session 10 of the UU curriculum *We Believe: Learning and Living Our Unitarian Universalist Principles*. Theodore Parker is also featured in Session 9 in *Travel in Time*. The hymnal *Singing the Living Tradition* contains words from Parker in No. 683, "Be Ours a Religion . . ."

Theodore Parker was born in Lexington, Massachusetts, on August 24, 1810, the eleventh child of John and Hanna Parker. Theodore's grandfather was Captain John Parker, who commanded the Minutemen on Lexington Common in 1774, where the first shots of the American Revolution were fired. Theodore Parker inherited the family fighting spirit; not only did he preach and write widely on the evils of slavery, he was active in the Underground Railroad, and in 1854 he organized a riot to break a captured runaway slave out of the Boston jail. (The riot did not succeed.) Parker also knew in advance of John Brown's plans to raid Harper's Ferry for guns.

Parker also entered into spirited controversies about the true nature of Christianity with more conservative members of the Unitarian clergy. In his well-known sermon, "The Transient And Permanent in Christianity," he said, "An undue place has often been assigned to forms and doctrines, while too little stress has been laid on the divine life of the soul, love to God, and love to man." His firm stance on this topic greatly influenced the eventual shaping of the denomination and its adherence to principles of freedom and tolerance.

Theodore Parker suffered from tuberculosis. He traveled to Europe for rest and study, but became ill and died in Florence, Italy, on May 10, 1860. His tombstone reads, "His name is engraved in marble, his virtues in the hearts of those he helped to free from slavery and superstition."

MARIA MITCHELL

∽

(1818–1889)

An Infinity of Questions

Once there was a little girl named Maria (*pronounced Mar-EYE-ah*), who was full of questions. When she was two she asked, "What?" What is that, and what is this, and what are those, and what are these? Her parents answered as best they could. "That's a dog, and this is a cat, and those are the dog's whiskers, and these are the cat's toes." Her parents gave her lots of answers, but she always had more questions.

When Maria was three, she started to ask, "How?" How does this work, how does that happen, how do we know how it goes?

Her parents tried to answer as best they could. "Boiling water makes steam, and steam pushes the lid of the teakettle, and we know because . . . well, because we do."

"But how?" Maria wanted to know. "How do you know?"

"Well, because . . . because we look at it, and we wonder, and we do experiments to find out the answers. You can do experiments, too."

When Maria was four, she started to ask, "Why?" Why do boats float, and why does it get dark at night, and why do cats have fur, and why do people wear clothes? Her parents tried to answer as best they could, but no matter how many answers they had, Maria always had more questions. She asked questions at home, she asked questions at school, she asked questions at the Quaker church where her family belonged. She asked questions of everyone she met—hundreds of questions, thousands of questions, millions of questions, an infinity of questions from one little girl.

Maria had an infinity of questions, and she also loved the infinity of the stars. In the evenings, she and her father would climb the stairs to the top floor of their house in Nantucket, Massachusetts, by the sea. Then they would climb up a ladder to get to the roof. On the roof was a small platform with a railing around it, called a widow's walk. From the top of the house Maria could see far out to sea . . . and far above her to the stars—hundreds of stars, thousands of stars, millions of stars, an infinity of stars and one little girl. "I love the stars," she told her father, and they would look through a telescope to see farther into the sky.

Then Maria would start to ask questions. "Where do stars come from? How old are they? Why do they shine? How many are there? How far away are they?"

Some questions her father could answer. Some he could not. So Maria set out to find out the answers for herself. She studied hard and read many books and did experiments, and she became an astronomer, a person who studies the stars. When she was twenty-nine she discovered a comet, which was named the Mitchell Comet, after her. The King of Denmark gave her a medal for discovering the comet. In 1848 she was named a member of the American Academy of Arts and Sciences, which had never had a woman member before.

But Maria was still full of questions. "How do we know God exists? Is all of the Bible true? Why are we here?" Some people gave her answers, but when Maria asked, "How do you know?" they answered only "Because we do," or "Because we read it in a book, and so that's the way it is, and we shouldn't ask anymore." Maria didn't think those were very good answers at all. But the answers to her questions weren't to be found in books or by doing experiments, so Maria kept asking.

One day, she heard a talk by a Unitarian minister named William Ellery Channing. He didn't have the answers, either, but he said there was room for an infinity of answers to the infinity of questions, and the important thing was to wonder, not to know. Maria decided to join the Unitarian church because those words "woke up her mind."

All through her life, Maria Mitchell asked "What?" and "How?" and "Why?" She became a teacher so she could help other people answer their own questions. In 1865 she became a professor of astronomy at Vassar College, and she taught other people about the stars. Sometimes they found the answers to the questions. Sometimes they didn't. But Maria Mitchell was happy either way, because the most important thing is to wonder, not always to know.

More About Maria Mitchell

MARIA MITCHELL IS FEATURED in Session 11 of *We Believe* and on pages 31–37 of *The UU Kids Book*. The hymnal *Singing the Living Tradition* contains words from Mitchell in No. 537, "Our Whole System."

Maria was born on August 1, 1818, in Nantucket, Massachusetts. She became a Unitarian and purchased a pew at the Nantucket Unitarian Church on September 24, 1845. Fifteen years later, she became the first woman elected to the American Philosophical Society in 1869. In 1873, she helped found the American Association for the Advancement of Women and served as its president from 1874 to 1876. In 1873, she also went to the first meeting of the Women's Congress, which was attended by many women's rights activists: Elizabeth Cady Stanton, Susan B. Anthony, Lucy Stone, Dr. Elizabeth Blackwell, and Antoinette Brown Blackwell. Maria Mitchell retired from Vassar in 1888 because of poor health. She died on June 28, 1889, in Lynn, Massachusetts.

Her home and observatory on Nantucket Island are now museums. For more information, contact the Maria Mitchell Organization at www.mmo.org or write to the Maria Mitchell Association at 4 Vestal Street, Nantucket, MA 02554, or call (508) 228-9198.

A Bright Star

THOMAS STARR KING

(1824–1864)

A long time ago, when railroad trains were still brand new and the United States had only twenty-four stars on its flag instead of fifty, there lived a boy whose name was Starr. That may seem like an odd sort of name to us today, but his mother's last name had been Starr before she was married, and back then, children were often given their mother's maiden name as their middle name. Starr's full name was really Thomas Starr King, but there were lots and lots of boys named Thomas around, and so his family called him Starr.

Starr was bright, just like his name. He was bright in school, learning his lessons well. He was bright at home, helping out cheerfully and doing his chores without complaints—not too many, anyway. And he was bright at the Universalist church his family went to, where his father was a minister. Starr was always happy to help. He carried the hymnals, he polished the candle holders, and he helped dust the pews.

But most of all, Starr loved to ring the church bell. On Sunday mornings, bright and early, he'd climb the stairs to the bell tower. He'd grab the rope with both hands and pull! And then: *bong!* would go the bell, and up would go Starr. That rope would pull him right off his feet! And then down he'd come with a *thump*, and the bell would go *dong!* Then Starr would give that rope another pull, and *up!* he'd go again, even higher this time, and the bell would go *bong!*

Starr loved ringing that church bell. He loved other music, too. He loved singing, especially at church, where lots of people sang in harmony. Some sang high, some sang low, some sang in-between, but all the different voices worked together to create one glorious song.

Starr liked everything about church. "When I grow up," Starr said, "I'm going to be a minister in a church, just like my father." And Starr was. When he was twenty-one, he was a minister in a Universalist church. But then, when he was twenty-four, he changed churches. He became a minister in a Unitarian church. (Back then, the Universalists and the Unitarians were still separate. Starr was ahead of his time. He was a Universalist Unitarian over one hundred years before the rest of us became Unitarian Universalists.)

Some of his friends weren't happy to see him change. "Starr!" they said, "how can you leave Universalism?"

"I'm not leaving Universalism," Starr said. "I can be a Unitarian and Universalist at the same time. I'm just singing a different part. We all sing together to make one glorious song."

In 1860, when railroads went from state to state and there were thirty-three stars on the American flag, Starr left Boston, Massachusetts, and moved all the way across the country to San Francisco, California. His friends weren't happy to see him go. "Starr!" they said, "how can you move so far away?"

"I'm not leaving our country," Starr said. "I'm just moving to a different state. All the states work together to make one great nation. "But the year was 1860, and not everyone agreed. The Civil War was coming, and the nation was being torn apart, some states to the North and some states to the South. The stars were coming off the flag. California was in the West, and no one was sure which way it would go.

Thomas Starr King was sure that the states should stay together, "one nation, indivisible," and he set out to convince everyone in California of that, too. He was a minister at his church in San Francisco, and he preached there on Sundays, but he also traveled around the state and made speeches. He made speeches in towns and in mining camps, in great lecture halls and in canvas tents. He made speeches in front of thousands and thousands of people. He didn't convince all of the people, but he convinced enough, and in 1861 California voted to stay in the Union and to keep its star on the American flag.

"He saved California for the Union," said a general in the Union army, and that helped the North win the war. The people of California still remember him for that today. California put a statue of him in the Golden Gate Park in San Francisco and sent another statue to Washington, D.C. That statue of Thomas Starr King stands in the Hall of Columns in the Capitol Building, and you can go see it, if you ever go there. He has two mountains named after him: one in California's Yosemite National Park and one in New Hampshire's White Mountains. Both the Unitarians and the Universalists still remember him, and we've set his name on the school where some of our ministers go: the Starr King School for the Ministry in Berkeley, California.

So you may hear his name from time to time, and now you know why: Thomas Starr King was a bright and shining star.

More About Thomas Starr King

THOMAS STARR KING IS featured in Session 23 of *Around the Church, Around the Year*. He is author of the famous quote "The one [Universalist] thinks God is too good to damn them forever, the other [Unitarian] thinks they are too good to be damned forever."

King was born on December 17, 1824, in New York City. His family moved to Boston when he was ten, and his father became the minister of the Charlestown Universalist Church. A precocious child, King published his first sermon at the age of thirteen. King's father died when King was only fifteen, and he left school to support his family. While working at the Charlestown Navy Yard, he occasionally attended classes at Harvard College and was mentored by such notables as Hosea Ballou II, Edwin H. Chapin, and Theodore Parker.

King became a minister at his father's church at the age of twenty-one. Many parishioners remembered him from his boyhood, and because of that and his youth, at times he was not taken seriously. In 1848 King became the minister of the Hollis Street Unitarian Church and soon after married Julia Wiggin. In 1850 he was awarded an honorary Master of Arts from Harvard. He lectured widely to supplement his income, and became well known. His travel essays on New Hampshire were gathered into the book *The White Hills: Their Legends, Landscape, and Poetry*, which was published in 1859. During his eleven years at the Hollis Street church, its membership increased fivefold and its financial status became secure.

In April 1860, seeking a wider challenge, he arrived in San Francisco and became the minister at the Unitarian church on Stockton Street. He soon became active in politics, campaigning on Lincoln's behalf during the 1860 election. Lincoln carried the state by a narrow margin. During the next year, King continued his political speeches and helped elect Republicans to the state senate, who voted not to secede.

But the Civil War was far from over. In addition to being a pastor at his church, King organized fund-raising for the United States Sanitary Commission, a civilian organization that oversaw the health and medical care of the United States Army. By the end of the war California had donated 1.5 million dollars, one-quarter of all the money received by the Sanitary Commission.

Weakened by his exhausting schedule, King contracted diphtheria and died on March 4, 1864. His casket, draped with the American flag, was placed in front of the altar of his church, and twenty thousand people came to pay tribute. The California state legislature closed for three days in mourning, and flags were set at half-staff.

FRANCES ELLEN WATKINS HARPER

(1825–1911)

Nearly two hundred years ago, a little girl was born in the city of Baltimore near the Chesapeake Bay. Her name was Frances Ellen Watkins. When Frances Ellen was born, in 1825, there weren't any cars and only a very few trains. When people wanted to go somewhere, they either rode horses or walked, or they might go for a ride in a carriage or travel the oceans in a tall-masted ship with white sails.

On the day that Frances Ellen was born, her mother said, "Frances Ellen, you are the most beautiful baby in the world, with your curly brown hair and your dark brown eyes and your soft brown skin." (Because that's the kind of thing that mothers say.)

Someday

And Frances Ellen said, "Gah." (Because that's the kind of thing that babies say.)

Then her mother said, "Frances Ellen, you are also the luckiest baby in the world, because we are not slaves. You have been born free!"

And Frances Ellen said, "Gah," because she was only a baby and she didn't understand what "free" meant. She didn't understand what "slave" meant. She didn't know that in 1825, slavery was legal in the southern parts of the United States of America, including the city of Baltimore. She didn't know that people with dark skin (brown skin like hers) could be bought and sold. She didn't know that children—even little children—could be taken away from their mom and dad, and they would never see each other again. She didn't know that slaves had to work hard all day, every day, and never got paid and were never allowed to leave. She didn't know that sometimes slaves were beaten or made to wear chains, or didn't have good food to eat or good clothes to wear. She didn't know that slave children often didn't have any toys, not even one. Frances Ellen was only a baby, and she didn't know about any of that.

But her mother knew. "Someday," her mother said, kissing the curly brown hair and looking into the dark brown eyes and touching the soft brown skin, "someday everyone will be free. Someday."

When Frances Ellen was older, she went to school. One of the teachers was her uncle, William Watkins. He said to the class, "Children, you are very lucky to be here, and to be allowed to learn." The children all nodded, serious and quiet, because even though they were only five and six years old, they already knew.

They knew that it was against the law for an enslaved person to learn how to read and write. They knew that most schools didn't let dark-skinned children—even free dark-skinned children—in. Frances Ellen and all the other girls were twice as lucky, because they knew that many schools wouldn't let girls in, only boys.

"Someday," William Watkins said, "someday all children will be allowed to learn, black and white, girl and boy. There will be schools for everyone. Someday." Then he smiled at them and opened his book. "But you, lucky children, can start learning today."

And Frances Ellen learned. She learned math and spelling and English and Latin and Greek, and she learned history and geography and music, but what she liked to do most of all was write. She wrote stories and poems and essays whenever she could. She studied hard and did her homework every day, because she knew she wasn't going to be able to stay in school for long. Her family needed money.

When she was fourteen, she left school and got a job. She lived with a Quaker family and helped take care of their children, and she cooked and cleaned. "Someday," Frances Ellen said to herself as she hung up the laundry on the clothesline or chopped carrots or scrubbed the floors, "someday, children will be able to stay in school longer and learn all that they can. Someday."

But even with chopping carrots and scrubbing floors, Frances Ellen still found time to read. The Quaker family she lived with let her use their library, because just like her uncle, they believed that everyone should be allowed to learn. Frances Ellen found time to write, too. She wrote stories and poems of her own. When she was twenty, her book *Autumn Leaves* was published and sold in bookstores. "A woman wrote this?" some people said. "A colored woman? No. That's impossible. It's too good."

"Someday," Frances Ellen said to herself, as she dipped her pen in the inkwell to write another poem, "someday, people will know that the work you can do doesn't depend on the color of your skin. People will know that both men and women can write. Someday."

But "someday" didn't look like it was coming any time soon, and so Frances Ellen decided she would help it along. She wrote poems and stories and sold over ten thousand books. She helped people who were running away from slavery by sending them money she'd made from her writing, even though helping them meant she could have been put in jail. She traveled from state to state, giving speeches to crowds of people—white people, black people, women and men—and she told them that slavery was evil and should be against the law. And finally, after more poems, after more speeches (by Frances Ellen and by many other people), after fifteen years and a Civil War that nearly ripped the country in two, finally, slavery was made illegal in every part of the land. Everyone was free.

Frances Ellen's mother's "someday" had finally come.

But there was still a lot of work to be done to make all of those other "somedays" happen. So, Frances Ellen got to work. She traveled to the southern parts of the United States and helped start schools for all those people who hadn't been allowed to go to school before. She worked with Susan B. Anthony and Elizabeth Cady Stanton to change the laws so that women would be allowed to vote, just like men.

She worked with the Women's Christian Temperance Union to try to stop people from drinking too much alcohol and then not having any money left for food. She worked with different churches to feed the hungry and teach the children.

Of all those churches, the one that she chose to join was the First Unitarian Church in Philadelphia. She became a Unitarian because she knew that Unitarians worked hard to make the world a better place, and to make those somedays come true.

Well, here we are. It's been nearly one hundred years since Frances Ellen died, and many of her "somedays" have arrived. It's not legal to keep slaves anymore in the United States. Women can vote. All children are allowed to go to school, and they can stay there until they're eighteen. We know that the work people can do doesn't depend on the color of their skin or whether they're a boy or a girl.

But there are still many "somedays" that haven't yet arrived. There are still people who are hungry. There are still children who don't have good schools. There is still a lot of work to be done. So, just like Frances Ellen, we Unitarian Universalists need to get to work and make those "somedays" come soon.

More About Frances Ellen Watkins Harper

FRANCES ELLEN WATKINS HARPER IS not featured in any UU curriculum, but her life has been dramatized in the play *A Brighter Coming Day*. Contact TBE Enterprises:

Tanya Bickley Enterprises, Inc.
P. O. Box 1656
249 Old Stamford Road
  (for express deliveries)
New Canaan, CT 06840
Tel.: 1-800-965-3347 Fax: (203) 966-6340
Email: tbickley@mindspring.com
Web site: www.bickley.com/harper.html

Frances Ellen Watkins was born on September 27, 1825, in Baltimore, Maryland, to free parents whose names are unknown. Her mother died in 1828, and Frances was raised by her aunt and uncle, the abolitionist William Watkins (father of William J. Watkins, an associate of Frederick Douglass). She received an excellent education at the Academy for Negro Youth, which was run by her uncle. She also absorbed many of her uncle's views on civil rights. At the age of fourteen, she found a job as a domestic in a Quaker household, where she was given access to their library and encouraged in her literary endeavors. Her poems appeared in newspapers, including Frederick Douglass's paper, and a volume of her poetry was printed in 1845 with the title *Autumn Leaves* (sometimes entitled *Forest Leaves*).

In 1850, the Fugitive Slave Law was passed, which allowed slave-catchers to pursue escaped slaves anywhere in the United States. No proof except the word of the slave-catcher was required that the person captured was indeed a slave. Anxious to leave the slave state of Maryland, the Watkins family moved to Pennsylvania, and Frances moved to Ohio, where she taught sewing at Union Seminary. (The principal of the school was the Reverend John Brown, who later became famous for his unsuccessful uprising at Harper's Ferry in 1859. Frances gave emotional support and comfort to Mrs. Brown during John Brown's trial and execution.)

In 1851, Frances moved to Pennsylvania. There, alongside William Still (chairman of the Pennsylvania Abolition Society and author of *The Underground Railroad*, which was published in 1872), she became active in the Underground Railroad, helping escaped slaves on their way to Canada. In 1854, while continuing to write and publish, she began her brilliant lecturing career. She was much in demand on the antislavery circuit and traveled extensively in the years before the Civil War.

In 1860, she married Fenton Harper, a widower with three children, and moved back to Ohio.

Their daughter, Mary, was born in 1862. Fenton died in 1864, and after the war was over, Frances toured the South, speaking to large audiences, encouraging education for freed slaves, and aiding in reconstruction.

In 1870, Frances and her daughter settled in Philadelphia. She joined the First Unitarian Church in that city, having become acquainted with Unitarians before the war, due to their staunch support of abolition and the Underground Railroad. Her friend Peter H. Clark, a noted abolitionist and educator in Ohio, had become a Unitarian in 1868.

With slavery a thing of the past, Frances turned her energy to women's rights, working with Susan B. Anthony and Elizabeth Cady Stanton to secure votes for women. Unlike Anthony and Stanton, Frances supported the Fourteenth and Fifteenth Amendments, which guaranteed the vote to black men, both freeborn and former slave. She reasoned that with the ever-present danger of lynching, someone in the African-American community needed to have a political voice and the possibility of securing legal and civil rights.

During the next few decades, she published numerous poems, short stories, and several novels, and she also remained active in social concerns. In addition to her membership at the Unitarian church, she worked with a number of churches in the black community of north Philadelphia near her home, feeding the poor, counteracting juvenile delinquen-cy, and teaching Sunday school at the Mother Bethel African Methodist Episcopal Church. In 1873, she became the superintendent of the "colored section" of the Philadelphia and Pennsylvania Women's Christian Temperance Union. In 1894 she helped found the National Association of Colored Women and became its vice president the following year. Along with Ida B. Wells, Frances wrote and lectured against lynching, and she was also a member of the Universal Peace Union.

Frances Harper died on February 22, 1911, nine years before women gained the right to vote. Her funeral service was held at the Unitarian church on Chestnut Street in Philadelphia, and she was buried in Eden Cemetery, next to her daughter, who had died two years before.

During the twentieth century Frances Harper's popularity as an author waned, and her books and poems went out of print. Her name was not mentioned in the history books, and so her role in social activism and politics was not learned. Her gravestone fell over and was covered by grass, and people assumed she had been buried without a marker. Many books and articles refer to her "unmarked grave" and relate it to her poem "Bury Me in a Free Land," whose last stanza is "I ask no monument, proud and high, / To arrest the gaze of passers-by; / All that my yearning spirit craves, / Is bury me not in a land of slaves."

However, she was not wholly forgotten. In September of 1992, approximately 150 African-

American UUs traveled to Philadelphia for a convention. To honor Frances Harper and to commemorate the one-hundredth anniversary of the publishing of *Iola Leroy*, one of her most famous novels, a new headstone was prepared. When a worker cleared the site for the installation, all were surprised to find the original headstone, forgotten but still enduring, just as Frances Ellen Watkins Harper's legacy has endured through the years, though we have not always remembered her name.

Frances Harper once wrote, "What matters it if they do forget the singer, so they don't forget the song," but it does matter, and so did she.

A Voice and a Vote

When Olympia Brown was little, girls weren't supposed to whistle. Girls weren't supposed to climb trees or run fast or catch frogs. But Olympia did; she did all those things, all those things and more. "You can do whatever a boy can do," her mother and her father told her, and Olympia knew it was true. She climbed trees and ran fast and caught frogs, and when she was in school, she answered the teacher's questions loud and clear.

"Little girls ought to be quiet," said one lady in town. "Little girls ought not to make themselves heard." But Olympia did. She had a voice, and she was going to use it, every day.

When Olympia Brown was a teenager, young women weren't supposed to go to college. Young women weren't supposed to leave home to go off and learn complicated things. But Olympia did; she did all those things and more. Olympia left home and went to Antioch College. She went to class and studied and learned all kinds of complicated things.

"Young women ought not to be in college," said one professor at that school. "But since they are here, they must read their reports. Young women ought not to give speeches from memory, like the men." But Olympia did. When it was her turn to present her report, she rolled up the papers in her hand and said each and every word, loud and clear. Olympia Brown had a voice, and she was going to use it, every day.

When Olympia Brown was in college, women weren't supposed to wear pants. Women weren't supposed to wear anything except very long dresses that came all the way down to their toes. But Olympia did. She wore dresses that came down only past her knees, and under them, she dared to wear pants! "Bloomers" the pants were called, after Amelia Bloomer, the woman who had created them a few years before.

"Women ought not to show their ankles in public!" exclaimed some of the men. "And women certainly ought not to wear pants!" But Olympia did. She wore her bloomers every day, no matter how much the men sneered.

When Olympia Brown was finished with college, women weren't supposed to be ministers. Women never stood up in front of a congregation and talked about God. But Olympia did; she did all those things and more. Olympia graduated from the Theological School at St. Lawrence University in 1863, and she was ordained as a

Universalist minister in June of that year, the second woman ever to be officially ordained by that church. She became the Reverend Olympia Brown.

"Women ought not to speak in public," said a minister at that time. "Women ought not to take the pulpit or discuss the nature of God." But the Reverend Olympia Brown did. During the next thirty-five years, she was a minister in five different congregations, and she visited other congregations, too. She took the pulpit in every single one, and she spoke on the nature of God and love, and she did an excellent job. Olympia Brown had a voice, and she used it, every day.

When Olympia Brown was born, women weren't allowed to vote. Women weren't allowed to have any say in who was elected president or senator or mayor of the town. But Olympia had something to say about that. Olympia had a lot to say about that.

She traveled all over the state of Kansas in a horse and buggy, giving speeches to convince people that women deserved the right to vote. She wrote hundreds of letters. She spoke to the representatives and senators in Congress. She marched in parades. Olympia and her friends worked hard to get women the right to vote. Olympia Brown had a voice, and she used it every day . . . every day for over fifty years.

And finally, when Olympia Brown was old, women were allowed to vote. In November of 1920, when Olympia was eighty-five years old, she voted for the very first time.

Olympia had always had a voice, and she'd used it to make sure that she—and all the other women in the United States—had a vote as well.

More About Olympia Brown

OLYMPIA BROWN IS FEATURED in Session 2 of the UU curriculum *We Believe*. The hymnal *Singing the Living Tradition* contains passages from her: Reading 569, "Stand by the Faith," and Reading 578, "The Great Lesson."

Olympia was born in 1835 in a log cabin in Prairie Ronde, Michigan. Her father, Asa Brown, built a school house on his property so that the children in the area could have a school. Her family were Universalists from Vermont. Olympia's mother, Lephia, believed strongly in women's rights, and Olympia's aunt and uncle were part of the Underground Railroad.

Olympia pursued both her education and her ministerial career with determination, even in the face of repeated discouragement and rebuffs. She served Universalist churches in Marshfield and East Montpelier, Vermont; Weymouth, Massachusetts; Bridgeport, Connecticut; and Racine, Wisconsin. From 1893 to 1898, she was a part-time minister in several Wisconsin towns.

In 1873 she married John Henry Willis but retained her own name. They had two children, Henry Parker Willis in 1874 and Gwendolyn Brown Willis in 1876. Both Henry and Gwendolyn became college professors.

Olympia became actively involved with women's suffrage in 1867, when Lucy Stone persuaded her to go to Kansas for a four-month speaking tour. In 1882, Olympia became president of the Wisconsin Woman Suffrage Association and held that post for nearly three decades. Convinced that a national constitutional amendment was necessary to gain the vote, instead of going state by state, she helped found the Federal Suffrage Association in 1892, serving as vice president and later president. She was a charter member of the Congressional Union in 1912, which later became the National Women's Party. With hundreds of other women, she picketed the White House day after day in 1917. After the Nineteenth Amendment was passed and the long struggle for the vote was over, Olympia campaigned for world peace. She died in Baltimore in 1926.

(1848–1928)

A clear-glass lightbulb can be shown at the beginning, or handed around if the audience is old enough to be careful. The four lines of the poem in the story needn't be memorized; reading them from a piece of paper can add a bit of drama.

A Longer Lasting Light

n 1879, when Thomas Alva Edison first showed his new electric lightbulb to people, they said, "Ohhhhh!" They'd never seen anything like that before. The lightbulb glowed, quiet and steady. It didn't flicker like a candle. It didn't make noise like an arc lamp. It didn't need refilling like a kerosene lantern. You just pushed a button or flipped a switch, and then—like magic!—the electric lightbulb glowed. People even called Thomas Edison a wizard, because he had invented such a magical thing.

People wanted that kind of magic in their own homes. They wanted to be able to flip a switch and have light, just like that! No more dripping candle wax. No more noisy sparks. No more worrying about fires. No more smelly kerosene.

But, there was one problem. Mr. Edison's lightbulb worked fine the first time it was turned on. It worked fine the second time, too. But after a few days, people didn't say, "Ohhh," when they turned it on. They said, "Uh-oh," because the lightbulb didn't light anymore. Thomas Edison's lightbulb used carbon thread for a filament—that little curly line inside the lightbulb—and the carbon thread lasted only about forty hours before it burned out. Once the filament burned out, the lightbulb would never work again. People would have to buy a new lightbulb. And a few days later, they'd have to buy another lightbulb, and then another one after that, and another one after that.

Nobody wanted to buy lightbulbs all the time. They were expensive. So people gave up on the idea of having electric lightbulbs in their homes, and kept on using candles and kerosene lamps.

But a man named Lewis Howard Latimer didn't give up on the idea of electric lightbulbs. Instead, he decided that he would make a longer-lasting light, a light that people could afford to buy.

It wouldn't be easy; he knew that. Many other people all over the world—very smart people such as scientists, inventors, and engineers—had been trying for years to make a longer lasting lightbulb that didn't cost a lot of money, and they hadn't found a way.

Now, Lewis Latimer had never gone to college. He didn't have a degree in engineering or physics or chemistry or anything like that. In fact, he'd hardly gone to school at all, only a few years of elementary school. Before he was born, his mother and his father had been slaves in Virginia. They had escaped from slavery and gone to Boston in the North, and so Lewis and his brothers and sister had all been born free. But the Latimer family was poor, and Lewis had had to get a job when he was only ten. He hadn't had much time for school.

But Lewis Latimer was smart. He was very smart. When he was a teenager, he had taught himself to do technical drawings, very careful and precise drawings of machines and inventions. He had helped Alexander Graham Bell draw diagrams of the telephone and get the patent on that. Lewis Latimer liked to do experiments, and he had also invented some things of his own. Even though he didn't have a college degree or a high school education, Lewis Latimer was a scientist *and* an inventor *and* an engineer. So Lewis Latimer decided he could figure out how to make a longer lasting lightbulb. And he did! He used his curiosity and his knowledge and his ingenuity to design a carbon filament that was baked in a special way and so lasted for a long time, hundreds of hours. Lewis Latimer received a patent for his carbon filament, which means that the United States government recognized that Lewis Latimer was the inventor, the very first person to create that carbon filament.

Now that lightbulbs could last for months instead of days, people wanted lightbulbs in their houses. They wanted them right away. Lewis Latimer went to Montreal, Philadelphia, New York, and London to teach people how to put electricity into their cities and homes. When he came back from London, Thomas Edison asked Lewis Latimer to work with him, and together the two of them invented many more amazing—even magical—things.

Electricity wasn't the only type of light that Lewis Latimer helped to create. He loved learning new things and teaching them to others. He shared the light of truth. He helped people who were hungry or who were poor, just like his family once had been. He knew that helping others was another way of sharing light, for in one of his poems he wrote

To love while we live
And give aid to each other
Is the sunshine of life
That turns night into day.

In 1908 Lewis Latimer helped to start a Unitarian church in the town of Flushing, New York. People are still going to that church, after nearly one hundred years. That Unitarian Universalist church—just like this Unitarian Universalist church—gives a long and lasting light. Lewis Latimer would be pleased.

More About Lewis Howard Latimer

LEWIS LATIMER IS MENTIONED on pages 4–9 of *The UU Kids Book* and is the subject of Session 20 in the UU curriculum *A Stepping Stone Year*.

In 1842, six years before Lewis Howard Latimer was born, his parents, George and Rebecca Latimer, decided to run away from their life of slavery in Virginia so that their first child could be born free. After a nerve-wracking journey of four days, during some of which George pretended to be Rebecca's owner, they arrived in Boston on October 8, 1842. Unfortunately, George was recognized almost immediately by a man who had known George and his master, James B. Gray, in Virginia. The man contacted Gray, who came to Boston on October 18 and had George Latimer arrested. Rebecca, eight months pregnant with their first child, went into hiding.

News of the arrest of an escaped slave spread quickly, and the antislavery groups mobilized. Nearly three hundred African-American men surrounded the jail where Latimer was being held to prevent him from being spirited away. Public meetings were held in Faneuil Hall, the same building the Sons of Liberty had often used during the American Revolution. William Lloyd Garrison publicized the case in his newspaper, *The Liberator*. William Francis Channing started a newspaper called *The Latimer Journal and North Star* with two of

his friends. Frederick Douglass, who had escaped from slavery only four years earlier, wrote and spoke on George Latimer's behalf. The strong outcry had its desired effect: George Latimer was set free the day before the hearing that would have determined if he should be sent back to Virginia as the property of James Gray. A black minister, the Reverend Samuel Caldwell, was concerned George Latimer might be arrested again, so the members of the Reverend Caldwell's church raised the sum of four hundred dollars and purchased George's freedom from Gray. George and Rebecca were reunited. Their son, George Jr., was born—free—in November of 1842.

The *Latimer* case was the first of several famous fugitive-slave cases tried in Boston. George's successful escape influenced the Fugitive Slave Act of 1850 and the *Dred Scott* decision of 1857, both of which strengthened the claims of owners on their runaway slaves. Ironically, their very strength hastened the coming of the Civil War, because the debate over slavery intensified and spread.

George and Rebecca were involved in the antislavery movement, but they were also trying to raise a family. After George Jr. came William, then Margaret, then Lewis Howard Latimer on September 4, 1848. The family struggled to make ends meet; George was skilled at doing many types of work, but jobs were scarce, especially for black men. And always there was the threat of slave-catchers finding Rebecca and taking her away or recapturing George. George's notoriety made it hard for them to hide, and the family moved frequently.

Lewis went to school occasionally, where he excelled, but most often he worked with his father, hanging wallpaper or helping in his father's barbershop. Lewis also had a job selling newspapers, including William Lloyd Garrison's *The Liberator*. When the Civil War started, Lewis was only twelve, but a few days after he turned sixteen, he joined the U.S. Navy as a cabin boy.

After the war was over, Lewis Latimer returned to Boston and found a job as an office boy in a patent lawyers' office, earning three dollars a week. He was fascinated by the drawings the draftsmen did of the many different devices, so he saved his money, bought some drawing tools, and taught himself how to draw. One day he volunteered to do a drawing. The draftsman laughed but let him try, and then was astonished when Latimer produced excellent work. The owner of the office was astonished, too, and impressed. In a few months Latimer was promoted from errand boy to draftsman and was earning twenty dollars a week.

These were good years for him. In 1873 he married Mary Wilson. He invented an improvement to the water closet and received a patent on it in 1874. The next year, Alexander Graham Bell, who happened to live near the lawyers' office, asked Latimer to help him apply for a patent for a new-fangled device called a telephone. Latimer made the drawings, and the patent was granted on March 7, 1876.

Latimer prepared patents for other electrical devices, and he invented a variety of devices, ranging from locking hat racks to book shelf supports. His improved carbon filament was patented in 1882, and soon electric lights revolutionized how people lived. He went to Philadelphia, London, Montreal, and New York City to help install the electric systems. To communicate better with the workers in Quebec, he learned French.

He moved to Brooklyn and then started working with Thomas Edison in 1884, both inventing and helping with patents. In 1890, Latimer wrote a book—*the* book, early engineers would say—about electricity, titled *Incandescent Electric Lighting: A Practical Description of the Edison System*. He was recognized as being one of the "Edison Pioneers," an elite group of twenty-eight men who worked with Edison before 1885.

Lewis Latimer was talented in both the sciences and the arts. He painted portraits, played the violin and the flute, and wrote poetry and plays. He spoke English, German, and French. He and Mary had two daughters: Emma Jeanette (born June 12, 1883) and Louise Rebecca (born April 19, 1890). Latimer enjoyed spending time with his children and, in time, his grandchildren. Jeanette married Gerald

Norman in 1911, and they had two children: Gerald Latimer Norman and Winifred Latimer Norman.

Lewis Latimer had always been active in social and political concerns. He was in contact with Frederick Douglass, Booker T. Washington, and W. E. B. Du Bois, and corresponded regularly with Richard Theodore Greener, the first African American to graduate from Harvard and the dean of Howard University's law school. "I am heart and soul in the movement," wrote Latimer to Greener in 1895, speaking of the fight for the rights of African Americans.

Latimer also helped other groups who were disadvantaged or discriminated against. In 1906, he began volunteer work at the Henry Street Settlement, teaching Eastern European immigrants to speak English. He taught a class on mechanical drawing, so that the newcomers could learn a useful skill.

In 1908, Lewis Latimer helped found a Unitarian church in the town of Flushing. Latimer had known of Unitarians all his life. Back in 1842, his parents had been helped by William Francis Channing, son of the Reverend William Ellery Channing, an organizer of the American Unitarian Association in 1825. The Unitarian belief in the importance of character, the toleration of different views, and the enthusiastic approach to learning matched Latimer's own views well. He and his wife and children were all active Unitarians. His granddaughter, Winifred Latimer Norman, was a leader in the Black Affairs Council and served on the board of the Unitarian Universalist Association. Latimer was an active member of the Flushing church until his health worsened in the 1920s. He died on December 11, 1928, at the age of eighty, and was buried next to his wife, Mary, in her hometown of Fall River, Massachusetts.

In the 1970s, the Henry Ford Museum in Dearborn, Michigan, created an exhibit to showcase Lewis Latimer's contributions in science and technology. In 1982, a street in Flushing was named after him. An elementary school and a housing development also carry his name. In 1988, his house at 64 Holly Street in Flushing was lifted off its foundations and moved one mile away to Leavitt Field, a city-owned athletic field. The house was converted into a museum of the history of Latimer and other African-American scientists.

The four lines of the poem are from "Keep in Touch with the World."

What We
Believe

Seven Stories of UU Principles

The Weight of a Snowflake

On a winter afternoon filled with blue shadows and white snow, a chickadee perched on the thin branch of a maple tree and watched the snowflakes fall.

A bright red cardinal flew over and landed nearby. "What-cha doin'?" chirped the cardinal.

"Watching snowflakes," said the chickadee.

The cardinal cocked his head to one side. "What for?"

"They're pretty. And each one is different! I haven't seen two that look the same."

"A snowflake is a snowflake, that's what I say," said the cardinal. "And they're cold. Me, I can't wait until spring. This winter stuff is for the mammals. They have fur on their toes." He lifted one foot and tucked it up under his feathers. "Us birds, all we got is scales."

The chickadee nodded, so that the little black cap on her head bobbed up and down, but she didn't say yes and she didn't say no.

White snowflakes fell all around them, and the blue shadows deepened to gray.

The cardinal put his foot down and hopped sideways on the branch to get a little closer to her. "What-cha doing now?" he asked.

"Counting snowflakes," said the chickadee.

The cardinal cocked his head to the other side. "What on sky for?"

"I was wondering how many snowflakes this branch would hold."

"Don't worry about it, that's what I say," said the cardinal. "Snowflakes don't weigh anything."

"Not anything?"

"Well . . . almost not anything. Snowflakes weigh next to nothing. They don't count for anything, and they're all the same." He clacked his strong curved beak once, twice, and then again. "You know what, little chickadee? You should find something else to do, that's what I say."

The chickadee nodded, so that the little black cap on her head bobbed up and down, but she didn't say yes and she didn't say no. After a minute, the cardinal clacked his beak once more, then flapped his strong red wings and flew away. The chickadee stayed where she was, perched on the thin branch of the maple tree and counting the snowflakes as they fell.

White snowflakes fell all around her, and the gray shadows slowly deepened to dusk. More snowflakes fell, each one different, each one beautiful. Some of them landed on that branch. Some of them landed on her. Snowflake after snowflake, each one weighing almost next to nothing, but each one counting for something.

Because, as the dusk deepened into darkness, and as the chickadee counted snowflake number ten thousand three hundred and three, that branch broke from the weight of the snow.

The chickadee fell with the branch, but only for a moment, for she flapped her wings and flew, up into the snowflakes that fell from the sky, each snowflake different, each snowflake beautiful, each snowflake counting for something, in its own way.

The Excruciatingly Scrupulous Twins

Once upon a time, not so very long ago, and in a place not so very different from our own, there lived a pair of twins named Tim and Tom, and they looked exactly the same: same hair, same eye color, same weight, same height. They wanted everything else in their lives to be exactly the same, too. So Tom and Tim were always fair with each other—excruciatingly, scrupulously fair.

Everything simply had to be fair. If Tom got a new pencil, Tim had to have a new pencil—same length, same color, same sharpness. If Tim got a new skateboard, Tom had to have a new skateboard. "Why don't you take turns?" asked their father, but taking turns wasn't the same as having your own, which meant it wasn't fair.

The twins were always careful to be fair—excruciatingly, scrupulously fair. In the morning at breakfast time, they counted every flake of cereal in their bowls, to make sure they had the same number. They each measured one-half cup of milk for their cereal. If Tim had three strawberries, Tom had to have three strawberries (even though Tom didn't really like strawberries), and the strawberries had to be exactly the same size. Oh, yes, they were fair.

"Why don't you share?" asked their mother, but sharing wasn't the same as having, and it certainly wasn't fair. The twins knew about sharing. They slept in the same bedroom, and they had to share that. So they did: excruciatingly and scrupulously. They put a line of tape down the exact center of the bedroom, to split the room exactly in half. On one side of the room were a bed, a dresser, and a desk. On the other side of the room were a bed, a dresser, and a desk: same kind, same size, same color. Luckily, the line of tape went through the center of the door, so they could both get in and out of the room without crossing over the line, even if they did have to turn sideways and not breathe and suck in their tummies to squeeze through. But one side of the room had a window and the other didn't, and so their bedroom wasn't fair.

And sometimes, no matter how hard they tried to make every single thing in their lives excruciatingly, scrupulously fair, they couldn't. Tom could run faster, and Tim could do cartwheels. Tom was good at math, and Tim was good at spelling. It didn't seem to make any difference how much they exercised or how hard they studied; they weren't identically the same, and that wasn't fair.

"Life isn't fair," said their father, but that wasn't . . . well, it wasn't fair! Things ought to be fair and even and equal.

Only things weren't.

And neither were their parents. "Go study your spelling," said their mom the night before a spelling test, but she said it only to Tom.

"Why doesn't Tim have to study?" Tom asked.

"Because he already knows how to spell all the words."

"That's not fair!" Tom said.

"You're right," his mom agreed. "But that's the way it is, so go study. You flunked the last spelling test, remember?"

Tom remembered. That had been the test with all those *I before E* words, except there were also a couple of tricky ones that were *"E before I."* Spelling was stupid, anyway. Who cared?

"Go study now," said his mom.

His mom cared. His dad cared. His teacher cared. Tom got out his spelling book and thumped it down on the table, but he didn't open it. He poked at the book with his pencil and stared gloomily at the wall. Tim sat down at the table, too, but he had a picture to color instead of homework to do. Tom made a face at him, and Tim made a face right back, so that was fair. But it didn't make Tom feel any better. He opened his book to the right page then poked at it with his pencil. This week it was words with silent *E*s. It was still stupid.

"You want help?" offered Tim.

Tom looked up in surprise. "You'd help me?"

"Well . . . yeah. Sure. If you want."

"But you already did your spelling homework. It won't be fair for you to have to do spelling again."

His brother shrugged. "That's okay. I don't mind helping you."

"Well, um, yeah. Thanks!" said Tim. "And hey, you know, two days from now we're going to have a math test, so tomorrow I can help you."

"Hey, yeah!" Tom said. "That's right!" Then he grinned. "That'll make it fair."

It would be fair tomorrow, but even more important than that, Tim decided, was that it was nice right now.

And maybe, Tim decided, maybe it was always more important to be nice than it was to be excruciatingly, scrupulously fair.

The Rooster Who Learned to Crow

There was once a farm in a valley that was practically perfect in every way, except that it had no rooster to crow at the crack of dawn, and so everyone was always late getting out of bed. The dog never woke up in time to fetch the newspaper for the farmer. The farmer never woke up in time to milk the cows before the sun rose. The cows never woke up in time to eat the grass when it was still wet with morning dew, which is when it is most tasty. Everyone was always late on that farm, and so everyone was always a bit cranky in the morning, and sometimes that crankiness lasted all day.

Until one day, a chicken arrived at the farm. Everyone was excited because she had four little yellow balls of fluff peeping and cheeping behind her. "Uh, pardon me, Mrs. Chicken," snuffled the pig, who was always exceedingly polite. "But would one of your chicks there happen to be, that is, might one be, a he?"

"Why, yes," answered Mrs. Chicken, and she pointed with the tip of her wing to the last chick in line. "That's my son."

"A rooster chicken!" squealed the youngest of the lambs, and all the other animals squealed (or whinnied or quacked or oinked), too. "We won't be late anymore! We have a rooster on the farm!"

But they didn't. Not yet. They had to wait for the chicks to grow up. And grow they did, from little yellow balls of fluff with legs to bigger yellow balls of fluff with legs. As the days passed, all the young chickens grew fine white feathers and bright yellow feet, and then—finally—young Mr. Rooster Chicken began to grow long swooping feathers on his tail.

"A tail, a tail!" squealed the youngest of the lambs. "Soon you'll be old enough to crow!"

"You look very handsome today, young Mr. Rooster," snorted the pig, who was always exceedingly polite. "A very fine looking fowl, if I so may say."

"Thank you," said young Mr. Rooster, with a bob of his head and a quiver of his cockscomb, but then he walked away, his long tail feathers drooping and his cockscomb down, too.

"What's wrong?" asked his friend, the gray-and-white cat who lived in the barn.

"Oh, nothing."

"Something's wrong," said his other friend, the yellow duck who swam in the pond. The pig came over to listen, too.

"Well," said the young rooster, scratching in the dirt with his strong yellow toes, "everybody's waiting for me to grow up and crow. I'm doing the growing-up part all right, but . . ."

"But what?" asked the cat.

"But I don't know how to crow! I've never even heard a rooster. I don't know what I'm supposed to do!"

"We shall help you," announced the pig, who was always exceedingly helpful as well as exceedingly polite.

"We will?" asked the cat, with every single one of his eyebrow whiskers raised. "How?"

"Yes, how?" quacked the duck.

"We shall teach him," said the pig. "You have heard a rooster crow before, have you not, Mrs. Duck?"

"Yes, I have!" said the duck. "I can show you." She flew to the top of the chicken coop nearby. Then she folded her wings back, tilted her bill up, and crowed. "Quack-a-whack a-whack a-whack."

The cat crouched down and flattened his ears.

"Hmmm," said the pig. "Thank you, Mrs. Duck, though that's not perhaps quite . . ."

"I hope not!" said the rooster, looking very much alarmed.

"I shall demonstrate," said the pig. "First, one must climb, though you will no doubt fly, to a high point." The pig climbed to the top of the manure pile. "Then, tilt your head back—Mrs. Duck did that part quite well—clear your throat and . . . crow." The pig tilted his head back and cleared his throat. "Oink a-snuffle, oink a-snort!"

The cat closed his eyes and shook his head.

"Hmmph!" said the duck, not at all impressed.

"Yes, well . . ." The pig climbed down from the manure pile. "That is not quite, uh, that is . . . it does sound a bit . . . you understand . . . with a real rooster . . ."

"I'll show you," said the cat, and he leapt to the top of the fence and curled his tail around his toes. He washed one paw and looked up at the sky. "Meow a-meow-a-meow-a-meow."

"Hmmph!" said the duck.

"Hmmm," said the pig.

"Oh, dear," said the rooster, looking even more alarmed.

"Maybe another chicken," suggested the duck, and they went to fetch one of the hens. But all she managed was "Cluck a-cluck a-cluck a-cluck!" The dog gave them "Woof a-woof a-woof a-woof!" The lamb went "Baa a-baa a-baa a-baa!"

The rooster sadly shook his head. "I'll never learn how to crow. I won't be any good at waking people up. Nobody will like me anymore."

"Sure we will!" said the cat. "I like you right now, and you've never crowed a day in your life." All the other animals agreed, with baas and moos and stomping of feet. "Besides," added the cat, "I don't want you waking me up. I like to sleep late."

"You will," said the rooster, as gloomy as a rainy day.

"I wonder," said the pig, "have you yourself ever tried to crow, Mr. Rooster?"

"Me?" said the rooster. "But . . ."

"You're more of a rooster than any of us," said the duck.

"And we'll like you no matter what you sound like," said the pig.

"Even if you don't make any sound at all!" said the cat.

And so the rooster decided to try. He flew up to the top of the chicken coop. He folded his wings back. He tilted his head. And he tried to make the same noises all his friends had tried to make before. Softly at first: "Cock-a-doodle-doo!" and then again, louder, "Cock-a-doodle-doo!" and then very loud indeed: *Cock-a-doodle-doo!*

After that, no one had any doubt that young Mr. Rooster knew how to crow, not even young Mr. Rooster himself.

◡

There is a farm in a valley that is practically perfect in every way. It even has a fine young rooster, who crows at the crack of dawn, and so everyone always gets out of bed exactly on time. The dog always wakes up in time to fetch the newspaper for the farmer. The farmer always wakes up in time to milk the cows before the sun rises. The cows always wake up in time to eat the grass when it is still wet with morning dew, which is when it is most tasty. Everyone is always wide awake on that farm, because they have a rooster whose friends helped him learn how to crow, just like this: "Cock-a-doodle-doo!"

∽

WE'RE FREE TO SEARCH FOR
WHAT IS TRUE.

The Race to the Top of the Tree

Deep in a green-shadowed forest, high on the spreading branches of the great oak trees, there lived a family of squirrels. It was a very large family, with parents and grandparents and great-grandparents, with dozens of aunts and uncles and nieces and nephews, and hundreds and hundreds of cousins. There were big squirrels and little squirrels, squirrels with light gray fur, squirrels with silver gray fur, squirrels with dark gray fur, and some squirrels with a touch of brown fur on their shoulders and on their backs. They were each a little bit different. But all of the squirrels had bright inquisitive eyes and plumes of feathery, fluffy tails that could be flicked this way and that way and from side to side.

And all of the squirrels—every single one of them, from the smallest to the largest, from the lightest gray to the darkest gray—loved to climb trees. They climbed up, they climbed down, they climbed out on the branches, to the very thinnest part, where the branches would sway up and down and Up and Down and UP and DOWN . . . like a seesaw, only faster and higher and a lot scarier.

But better than tree-climbing, and even better than tree see-sawing, was tree-racing. Every day—sometimes three or four or five times a day—the squirrels would hold races to see who could climb fastest, who could jump farthest, and who could climb highest of all. But since they were squirrels and squirrels are always hungry, sometimes they would stop racing to eat a nut, completely forgetting they were in a race at all! But that was all right, since they always had fun, whether they were eating or racing or just lying around being squirrels.

One morning, on a brisk autumn day when acorns were falling with a *plop!* and *platter!* all over the forest, and leaves came wifting and wafting slowly down, three squirrels were having a discussion about the best way to get to the top of the tree.

"Straight up the trunk!" said the dark gray squirrel, who was nibbling an acorn.

"But the trunk doesn't go all the way to the top," said the light gray squirrel, who was hanging upside down by her toes. "You have to go on the branches sometime."

"But when?" said the third squirrel, who had silver-gray fur touched with brown. "And which branch?" She looked up to the leafy canopy above.

"That big one, over there," said the dark gray squirrel.

"No, the crooked one, on that side," said the light gray squirrel.

"The big one!" said the dark gray squirrel again.

"The crooked one!" said the light gray squirrel, and they got to arguing with much chittering and cheeing and snipping of their teeth and snapping of their tails.

"This is silly," the silver-gray squirrel said finally, with a snap and a *flick!* of her own fluffy tail. "Stop talking about it and do it! Have a race!"

Both the light gray and the dark gray squirrel liked that idea, and other squirrels liked it, too. They gathered at the base of the great oak tree, dozens of them, for the Great Race to the Top of the Tree. Hundreds more came to watch. The racers waited for the start signal—ears perked, whiskers quivering, tails flicking just a little—and when the Great-Grandmother Squirrel of the Forest dropped an acorn and the acorn hit the ground, they were off!

Squirrels going this way, squirrels going that way, squirrels everywhere! They leapt for the trunk and dug in with their toes. Some—including, of course, the dark gray squirrel—raced straight up the tree trunk. Some ran up it going around and around, like climbing up a corkscrew slide, because that was more fun. Some squirrels didn't go up the trunk of the oak tree at all. Instead, they ran over to the big pine tree nearby and climbed up that, all the way to the top, and then made a daring leap across open sky to reach the tip of an oak branch fifteen feet away. There they clung, swaying up and down and Up and Down and UP and DOWN, until finally the branch stopped swaying and the squirrels could start climbing again.

Now, the great Oak of the Forest is a very tall tree, and it is a very long climb to the top. Many of the squirrels (since they were squirrels and squirrels are always hungry) stopped to eat an acorn or two along the way. Some never made it off the pine tree; they stopped there to nibble on pine cones. Some of the squirrels had so much fun going around and around the trunk of the oak tree chasing each other that they stopped worrying about the race at all.

But the dark gray squirrel did go up the big branch, and the light gray squirrel did go up the crooked branch. They went higher and higher, and the branches got thinner and thinner, and the wind grew stronger and stronger, and the ground got farther and farther away, and the sunshine grew brighter as they climbed above the leaves. Of all the squirrels, they were the only two who reached the very top of the tree, and they reached it at just about the same time.

"It's pretty up here," the dark gray squirrel said, holding on tight with all four paws as the very thin branches swayed to and fro in the very strong breeze.

"Yes, it is," the light gray squirrel said, holding on tight, too. "Ready to go down?"

"Yes!" said the dark gray squirrel. "Let's go get some acorns." So they did.

And the silver-gray squirrel? Why, she didn't climb the tree at all. She stayed down on the ground the whole time. "After all," she had said to herself, watching the other squirrels scamper away, "it doesn't really matter how far or how fast or which way you go, or even if you go up a completely different tree. There are lots of ways to get to the top of the tree, or to other parts of the tree, or to different trees altogether. In fact," she said, picking up an acorn between her two front paws, "you don't even have to climb any tree at all, because there are plenty of good things right down here on the ground, too."

t was a warm summer evening, in that glorious time between supper being over and having to get ready for bed, when the fireflies start to appear one by one, three children went outside to play.

"But what should we play?" asked Tabitha, who was the oldest of them all (by four months and two days). She had bright shiny braces and beads braided into her hair.

"Let's play tag," said Alex, who was the next oldest (by two months and fifteen days). He always wore his baseball hat sideways, and he always wore his T-shirt tucked in.

"Let's play hide-and-seek," said Shina, who was the youngest of the three. She

Playing Fair

had three braids in her long dark hair, two little braids in front on either side of her face and one bigger braid that hung down her back.

"Tag," said Alex.

"Hide-and-seek," said Shina.

"Tag."

"Hide-and-seek."

"Tag!"

"Hide-and-seek!"

"Stop it!" said Tabitha, stomping her foot and crossing her arms. "Let's vote."

Shina looked at Alex, and Alex looked at Shina, and then they both said, "Okay."

"We can have secret ballots and everything!" said Tabitha, and she ran inside her house then brought back paper and pencils and a shoe box with a skinny hole cut in the top.

Shina took her piece of paper and wrote "Hide-and-seek" in neat and careful letters. Then she folded her paper and put it through the skinny hole into the box. Alex and Tabitha were already done.

"Right! Now we count them," said Tabitha, and she took the lid off the box and unfolded each paper. "Tag, hide-and-seek, tag. It's two to one. Tag wins."

"Okay!" said Shina, and the three of them played tag until their parents called them inside to get ready for bed.

The next night, Tabitha brought the shoebox and they voted again. "It's two to one!" announced Tabitha. "Tag wins."

Shina sighed. "Okay."

Tag won the next night, too. And the night after that, and the night after that. "It's not fair!" Shina said. "But we voted on it," Alex replied, and that was true. And besides, they lived in a democratic country, and in a democracy, voting was the way to decide.

"It's still not fair," Shina muttered and so the next night, when tag won again, she decided not to play.

"Oh, come on!" said Tabitha. "Tag isn't fun with only two people."

"Tag isn't fun at all," Shina said darkly. "I'm tired of playing tag. I quit."

Tabitha looked at Alex, and Alex looked at Tabitha, and then they both looked at Shina, who wouldn't look at either of them at all. Tabitha jingled the beads braided into her hair. Alex turned his baseball hat so it pointed the other way. Then Alex said, "Well, maybe instead of voting all the time, we could take turns."

Shina looked up. "Take turns?"

"Yeah. Two nights playing tag, because there are two of us who like to play it, then one night playing hide-and-seek because there's one of you."

"We could start tonight!" said Tabitha. "We could even play hide-and-seek for a couple of nights in a row, because we haven't played it yet at all. How's that sound, Shina?"

"That sounds great!" Shina said. "I'm going to go hide!"

"Me, too!" said Alex. "That means you're It, Tabitha!" and he and Shina ran off to hide, while Tabitha closed her eyes and counted, sometimes slow, and sometimes a little too fast. When she got to one hundred, she yelled, "Ready or not, here I come!"

And on that warm summer evening, in the glorious time between supper being over and having to get ready for bed, as the fireflies appeared one by one, the three children played outside until their parents called them home.

A Lamp in Every Corner

Many years ago in the land of Transylvania, in a mountain valley watered by quick rushing streams and shadowed by great forests of beech trees, there was a village of small wooden houses with dark-shingled roofs. The people in the village were of the Unitarian religion, and they wanted a church of their own. A church set on the hillside, they decided, looking down upon the village as a mother looks down upon her sleeping child.

So all the people of the village labored long and hard to build themselves a church. The stonemasons hammered sharp chisels to cut great blocks of gray stone, then set the stones into stout and sturdy walls. The glaziers made tiny glass panes and fitted them neatly into the windows with leaded lines. The foresters sawed tall beech trees into enormous beams and laid the trusses for the ceiling, then covered the roof with close-fitting wooden shingles that wouldn't leak a drop of rain. The carpenters carved wood for the pair of wide-opening doors, setting them on strong pegs so that the doors hung straight and square. A bell was brought from a faraway city, then hoisted by ropes with a *heave* and a *ho* to the top of the tower. The weavers wove fine cloths for the altar table, cloths embroidered with flowers and edged with lace. The smiths hammered black iron into tall lamp stands and hammered thin bronze into shining oil lamps.

Finally, when the building of the church was done, the painting of the church could begin. The painters mixed bright colors: royal red and shimmering gold and brilliant blue, and everyone in the village—old and young, women and men, boys and girls— came to decorate their church. They painted flowers. They painted trees. They painted designs around the windows and different designs around the doors.

And at the end of the day, when it was finished—when their church was finally done—all the people of the village stood back to admire it . . . and then to sing, a song of happiness and praise. Their village had a church now, a church set on the hillside, looking down upon the village as a mother looks down upon her sleeping child.

"We will eat now!" announced an elder of the village, because everyone was hungry after their long day's work. "And later tonight, we will come back to pray."

So the people of the village went down the hillside to their homes and their suppers, all except one little girl named Zora and her father, who stayed behind. They had brought their own bread and cheese. They ate their food slowly, sitting on the grass on the hillside and admiring their new church with its strong stone walls, its tall tower, and its magnificent bell.

After they had eaten, they went back inside, opening those carved wooden doors to go into the gloriously painted sanctuary inside. "Oh, look, Father!" Zora cried, running from picture to picture, with her footsteps echoing off the stone walls. "See how pretty the church is!" She stopped in the center of church and twirled slowly around. "See how grand!"

"Yes, it is," said her father, looking around and nodding with pride. "Yes, it is."

"But, Father," she said suddenly, "we have not finished!"

"What do you mean?"

"There are tall iron lamp stands all along the walls, but there are no lamps! The church will be dark when the people come back."

"Ah no, little one," said her father. "The light of the church comes from its people. You shall see!" He rang the bell to call the people to worship, then took his daughter by the hand and led her back outside. They waited on the grassy hillside, next to their beautiful church of strong gray stone.

The sun had set behind the mountains, and night was coming soon. Yet in the growing darkness, tiny points of light came from many directions and moved steadily up the hill.

"Each family is entrusted with a lamp, little one," her father explained. "Each family lights its own way here."

"Where is our family's lamp?"

"Your mother is carrying it. She will be here soon."

The many lights moved closer together, gathering into one moving stream, all headed the same way, growing larger and brighter all the time. Zora's mother arrived, bearing a burning oil lamp in her hands. The father lifted Zora so she could set their family's lamp high in its tall iron stand. All around the church, other families were doing the same. Soon the church was ablaze with light in every corner, for all the people of the village had gathered to pray and to sing.

All through the worship service, Zora watched the lights flicker and glow. She watched her family's lamp most of all. When the service was over, her father lifted her high. She took the shining bronze lamp from the lamp stand. Its curved sides were warm and smooth in her hands. Her mother carried the lamp home, with the flame lighting the way.

The lamp flame lit their house when they returned home. Zora washed her face and got ready for bed by the light of that flame. "Mother," Zora began, as she climbed into bed and lay down.

"Yes, little one?" her mother asked, tucking the red wool blanket around Zora's shoulders.

"Father said the light of the church comes from its people."

"Yes."

"But also, the people take their light from the church!" Over on the table by the fireplace, the shiny bronze lamp was still burning. "And we have that light every day."

"Yes, indeed," said her mother. "And even when we are not in church, even when the lamp is not lit, we carry the light of truth in our minds and the flame of love in our hearts to show us the right way to be. That light—the light from truth and love—will never go out."

"Never?" asked Zora.

"Never," said her mother. "And this bronze lamp will last for many, many years. When you are grown, we will give the bronze lamp to you, and when your children are grown, you will give the lamp to them, and all of you will carry it back and forth to church every time."

"But there is only one lamp," Zora said.

"So make another, and let the light grow. And someday, tell your children to make more lamps, too. And now goodnight," her mother said and kissed Zora once on this cheek and once on that cheek and once on the forehead. Zora closed her eyes and drifted into dreams, while her mother looked down upon her sleeping child.

The years passed; Zora grew. The bronze lamp came into her care. She kept it polished and clean, and when the bell rang out across the valley to call the people to worship, she carried the lamp back and forth to the church on the hillside, the flame always lighting her way. When the time came, she made more lamps and gave them to her children, who made more lamps and gave them to their children, and so it went, on through the years, even until today.

And always, the light of truth and the flame of love from that Unitarian church on the hillside continued to grow and show them—and us—the way.

And It Is Good

On a day not so very long ago, in a place not so very far away, a grass seed lay waiting. All through the cold, dark days of winter the seed waited, covered by a blanket of earth. In the spring, when the air was warmed by the sun and the land was watered by the rain, the seed began to grow. It grew roots deep into the earth. It grew a delicate pale green shoot up into the air. As the days went by, the shoot grew into a firm stalk, which waved in the hot summer breeze. It grew bright green leaves that opened to the sunshine, and then grew darker green as more days went by.

It grew and grew and grew, until the seed was a tall stem of grass and was ready to make seeds of its own. In the fall, when the nights turned cool and the leaves on the trees flamed red and orange and gold, the grass plant knew it would soon be dying, and so it set free its seeds. They traveled on the wind, above field and stream and hill. Some of them slowly settled to the ground in a meadow, where they lay waiting, covered by a blanket of earth. And it was good.

Now in that place not so very far away, a small field mouse was looking for food. Winter was coming, and the mouse was hungry. He went here and he went there, sniffing his way through the meadow, ears perked, eyes open, whiskers quivering, careful and cautious always, for there are many creatures that will eat a mouse. And as he sniffed and nibbled and then sniffed some more, he found a few of those grass seeds that lay covered by the blanket of earth. So he dug them up—*scritch, scratch!*—and he ate them. And it was good.

Now in that place not so very far away, a snake was hunting. Winter was coming, and she was hungry. She went here and she went there, gliding through the faded fallen leaves from the trees, and tasting the air with flickerings of her forked tongue. She tasted the scent of mouse, and followed the scent to the meadow. After a while, she found him. So she caught him—*quick, snap!*—in her jaws, and she ate him. And it was good.

Now in the sky, high above that place not so very far away, a hawk was searching. Winter was coming, and the hawk was hungry. He went here and he went there, soaring on the wind with outstretched wings, looking down to the earth far below. And at the edge of the meadow, he saw the snake gliding through faded fallen leaves. So he folded his wings and he plummeted, straight down to the ground, and he caught that snake—*snatch, catch!*—in his fiercely curved claws, and he ate her. And it was good.

The days went by in that place not so very far away. The sun no longer warmed the air. Instead of rain, snow fell. The last of the leaves fell from the trees. The grass froze and died. Winter had come.

The hawk soared on outstretched wings, lifted high by the winter winds, hunting. But he was an old hawk. His wings did not beat so strongly as they used to. His eyes did not see so clearly. His hunts did not go well. One day, he plummeted to earth for the last time, and he died. And it was good.

The body of the hawk lay on the ground all winter long, covered by snow. When spring came, the sun warmed the air, and the rain watered the land. Flies buzzed in the air. Ants scurried over the ground. Spring was here, and they were hungry. The ants and the flies found the body of the hawk. The flies laid their eggs in it, and the eggs hatched into maggots. The days went by, and the body of the hawk slowly disappeared, the flesh and feathers eaten by ants and maggots, the bones chewed on by small animals, and whatever was left provided food for bacteria and mold. In just a few weeks, the body of the hawk had completely melted back into the earth. And it was good.

Now in the earth where the hawk had melted, a seed lay waiting. As spring turned into summer, and as the sun warmed the air and the rain watered the land, the seed began to grow. It shot a pale green shoot up into the air. It pushed roots deep into the earth, which was made up from the body of the hawk, who had eaten the snake, who had eaten the mouse, who had eaten the seeds. And it was good.

So remember, in that place not so very far away, and in all the places all around, there is sun, and there is rain. There are seeds and mice and snakes and hawks. There are ants and maggots and bacteria and mold. There are crocodiles and humans and plankton and daffodils and mushrooms. They all eat from each other. They all live, and they all die.

And it is all good.

How to Tell a Story and Create a World

To tell a story is to create a world. It might be a world where dragons speak or cows fly, a world of green-shadowed oak trees or of glass and steel skyscrapers, a world of magic or a world of the mundane. You can create such a world in just a few minutes with your voice, your hands, and your words.

But . . . I've never told a story before.

Sure you have! We all have. We tell stories all the time: about the traffic, about the spilled milk at the grocery store, about our boss or our teacher from third grade, about a fish we caught or a bird we saw. We start telling stories at the age of two or three ("And there was a dog with a skirt and a cat on a wire and a most biggest elephant and a clown at the circus!"), and we keep on telling stories through the years. It's the way that we tell the stories that makes them either a simple recounting of the facts or a vivid recreation that lets the listener see, hear, and believe.

To make a story vivid, to make it *see-able*, storytellers choose words that create pictures in the mind's eye. To say, "There was a bird in a tree" tells us that and not much more, but to say, "High on the topmost branch of the darkest fir tree in the forest, a lone chickadee perched and sang" opens a window to a story-world. The next time you find yourself telling someone about some small occurrence in your day, try adding a few descriptive words. Or, close your eyes and visualize a scene (a day at the seashore, a child in springtime, a whale breaching the surface), and then describe it in words.

When creating descriptions, appeal to all of the senses—sight, hearing, taste, touch, and smell. It wasn't simply "a car" that didn't move when the light turned green; it was a blue truck with a broken fender and a coat hanger for an antenna. It wasn't simply "a noise" that scared everyone at the picnic; it was a thunderous boom overhead. Not just "good" cake, but chocolate cake, dense and moist and worth licking off the plate. Not just "rough," but furrowed and peeling like tree bark under your hand. Not just a "spicy scent," but cinnamon with a hint of nutmeg.

Those five senses aren't our only ones. We have a sense of balance, a sense of rhythm, a sense of movement. Were you as dizzy as a cat in a washing machine? Were your toes tapping to the drumbeat? Were you seasick on the boat? Share the details with your listeners, and they will share in the tale you tell.

Of course, stories are more than just descriptions, however vivid those might be. Stories need characters, some sort of plot, a sense of movement. They need a beginning and an end.

I'm not sure I can remember all of that.

You remember more than you realize, and you can remember all that you need. Stories aren't like poems that need to be recited word for word, and they're not like three-hundred-page books with long paragraphs and complicated dialogue. If someone asks, "What happened in the movie?" we can usually name the characters, summarize the plot, and even remember a line of dialogue or an unusual costume or scene. That's all that most storytellers remember about their stories. They make up the rest of it as they go along. They use short sentences so the listeners don't get confused. Often, storytellers add a repeating phrase throughout the story, much like a chorus in a song.

Let's look at a familiar folktale, "Goldilocks and the Three Bears." The names of the characters are Goldilocks, Papa Bear, Mama Bear, and Baby Bear. The plot is straightforward: a little girl goes for a walk and gets into things she shouldn't, then is discovered. We probably have a few vivid phrases or images in our minds: "Who's been eating my porridge?" and "This one is too hot! Too cold! Just right!" We know the bare bones of the story, and that's all we need to get started.

No, it isn't! What do I do with my hands? Should I use different voices for the different characters? Do I sit? Do I stand?

These choices are entirely up to you. Some storytellers prefer to sit. They might use changes in their tone of voice and the occasional hand gesture to emphasize the story. Others walk about and physically act out their story, hopping like squirrels or stomping like giants. Some stories will lend themselves to quiet voices; others are full of sound and fury. Very few stories, however, sound like deadly dry lectures from school. Expressiveness and animation can help make a story livelier, so don't be afraid to exaggerate facial expressions or make odd sounds. Experiment with different postures and gestures. Try squeaky voices, deep voices, slow voices. Consider using props or puppets or musical instruments. Try anything you want, just to see how it works. You don't have to use it; this is practice.

One physical thing that you absolutely must do is breathe. You need oxygen to think. You need air in your lungs to speak. When we're nervous, we sometimes hold our breath or breathe shallowly. Remind yourself to breathe deeply and fully between sentences. Don't be afraid to take your time. Pausing can add emphasis to your story, and silence is as much a part of a story as sound.

Even for a storyteller, one of the prime directives in sharing any story is "Show, don't tell." Instead of saying, "He scuffed his toes in the dirt," scuff your own toes in the dirt. Instead of saying a line of dialogue followed by "he said sternly," be stern. Fold your arms across your chest, lower your eyebrows, take on a serious tone of voice, and then say that line of dialogue. Actions speak louder than words, and storytellers have both at their disposal.

Always remember: there is no wrong way to tell a story. You should tell the story in a way that feels right for you. Imitating another storyteller's methods or doing something because you think you "ought to" may make you feel awkward or constrained. Be yourself. Play with the story and have fun.

Which story should I tell?

For the very first story you tell aloud, you might consider choosing a story you already know instead of one of the stories from this book, so that you can concentrate on learning how to tell a story instead of learning the story itself. Perhaps your children have a favorite nursery tale. Perhaps you have a childhood favorite. It's important to pick a story you like. Your enthusiasm (or lack of enthusiasm) will shine through.

All right, I've picked a story I like. How do I start? What do I say first?

That's an excellent question, because the first thing you say "sets the stage." A simple and effective way to start is with the title: "This story is called 'Goldilocks and the Three Bears.'" Naming stories helps people (and storytellers) remember which story is which.

After you've named the story, you can pause before saying the opening line. This line will "open the curtain" and reveal what's on the stage. The tone of it will tell the listeners if the story is spooky or funny, fantasy or fable, happy or sad. It usually tells "where" and "when" the story happens. It may introduce the main character. There are many classic opening lines.

> *Once upon a time . . .*
> *I sing of arms and the man . . .*
> *A long time ago (in a galaxy far, far away) . . .*
> *Deep in the forest . . .*
> *In a hole in the ground there lived a hobbit . . .*
> *When giants walked and dragons flew . . .*
> *In a town not much different from our own . . .*

The opening line should fit the story, but it doesn't need to be any more complicated than the time-honored "Once upon a time, there was a little girl."

All right, I said the opening line. Now what?

Now you tell the story. But don't panic; remember, there is no "proper" way to tell a tale. You can't get it wrong. You are telling the story, in your own words and in your own way. Stories change. They change from storyteller to storyteller, from audience to audience, from moment to moment. The story you tell tomorrow will not be the same story you told yesterday, and that's fine. That is the way storytelling is supposed to be: flexible, innovative, and yours. So feel free to improvise, add, change, emphasize, or embellish as you see fit.

Of course, you still have to tell the story. You still have to get your character from point A to point B. Happily, classic folktales are designed to be easy to remember. They contain repetition, often in groups of three, to give the story structure and to help you remember what comes next. Characters may have a journey out and then a journey back, passing the same set of landmarks both times. These repetitions are "hooks" that you can hang your story on. They're the arrows pointing you in the right direction in case you get lost. Also, folktales are often short, perhaps only a few minutes, and short stories have simple plots.

Let's go back to "Goldilocks and the Three Bears." We've already started with "Once upon a time, there lived a little girl." What do we know about this little girl? She has gold hair and her name is Goldilocks. Add a sentence to your opening line.

"Once upon a time, there lived a little girl. She had hair as gold as the butter spread thick on a piece of bread, and so her parents called her Goldilocks."

What happens next? Goldilocks goes for a walk in the woods. That's the plot; we can add some details and spin that one line into a paragraph.

"Early one fine morning, when the mist was still curling around the dark trunks of the tall pine trees, Goldilocks picked up her walking stick and said goodbye to her mother and father. She shut the door and set off down the path that led away from their cozy little cottage, across the pasture where the cows wandered in the clover, and then deeper and deeper into the dark forest of pines."

This version of the story takes place in the morning, in a forest of pine trees, and Goldilocks is carrying a walking stick. The story could just as easily have started in the afternoon, in a forest of oak trees, and Goldilocks could be carrying a woven basket. The details create the world, and that world is yours. Maybe you want Goldilocks to have hair as yellow as sunshine on daffodils. Maybe you want to show her arguing with her parents about doing her chores before she goes. Maybe you want to switch the setting from a forest to a modern town and change the bears into people. Maybe you want the bears to try to eat her at the end of the story, and she fights them off with her walking stick. All of those ideas are fine. You can do any of them. The story is yours.

Visualize the scenes of the story; make them *see-able* in words. Is it cloudy or sunny? Is the cottage brightly painted or plain wood? Think about how Goldilocks feels. Defiant? Bored? Curious? Think about how the bears feel when they find her in Little Bear's bed. Outraged? Frightened?

Amused? Imagine your way through the story from beginning to end.

I got through the story, but how do I end it? It just kind of hangs there.

Giving a story a clear finish is just as important as giving it a clear start. "Once upon a time . . ." is a traditional opening, just as "They lived happily ever after" is a traditional ending. Other endings might suit a story better.

At last they were home.

And so they went to sleep, curled up in front of the fire.

And there he lived and there he stayed, and some say he's there still.

And she never again went into the bears' cottage without knocking.

People will recognize and respond to those openings and endings, just as they recognize and respond to traffic signals. With the opening, they'll settle back to listen. With the closing, they'll realize they can stop being an audience and start talking to each other again.

The closing line ends the story, but the storytelling session continues until you make your "exit." Just as at the beginning, stating the title is simple and effective: "And that is the story of 'Goldilocks and the Three Bears.'" Stating the title at both the

beginning and at the end follows the adage "Tell them what you are going to tell them. Tell them. Then tell them what you just told them."

Some storytellers add their own signature phrase at the end of every story they tell, much as an artist signs a painting. Ruth Sawyer said, "Take this story and may the next one who tells it make it better." Some say, "And so I heard it, and so I share it, and so may you share it someday." Ending with "Thank you for listening. It is time to go to your religious education classes now" works well, too.

I have a beginning, a middle, and an end, but I'm still worried about forgetting parts.

Learning a story does take practice, and practice means repetition. It's not so much a matter of memorizing the story with your head, as it is learning the story by heart. When you feel the story, when it's more than just words strung together, you can't forget it. It's a part of you.

Some people like to write their version of the story down, either in detail or in outline form. Some people read their version over and over, maybe reading it aloud. Other people write on note cards and flip through them as they practice. Others never refer back to the written word; the act of writing itself helped them to remember. Still others never write at all; they prefer to act out the story with physical movements. Some people use audiotapes and listen to their voice. Try different ways and find one or more that works for you.

When you feel that you have the story learned by heart and not only with your mind, put yourself in a comfortable environment and tell the story. Actually say the words aloud, all of them, from "Once upon a time . . . " to ". . . and she ran back home and never went into the bears' cottage again." It's all right to refer to your notes in the middle of telling; this is a practice session. Your comfortable environment might be in a car or in the shower. It might be in front of a wall or in front of a mirror. Some people videotape their storytelling.

Perhaps talking to yourself feels strange. Perhaps you would be more comfortable with a listener—a sympathetic one, of course! Young children are usually thrilled to be told a story, and they make very appreciative audiences. If you don't have young children at home, ask a friend or a neighbor if you can borrow one for a few minutes, or drop by the religious education classes on Sunday.

You can also ask an adult to listen. If you don't want any critiquing, good or bad, tell them so. If you'd like to hear only the good, let them know that, too. If you feel ready for the comments about what you might do better, you can ask ahead of time that they be given in a constructive manner. Maybe the comments could be written down instead of spoken, if that helps you to accept what the person has to say.

Chose a listener who you know has tact, and always remember: the main purpose of this first telling of the story is to help you learn how to tell a story. If the audience enjoys it, that's a wonderful bonus. Be glad! If the audience didn't enjoy it, that doesn't mean that the exercise was a failure. It means that you have succeeded in telling your first story, and that you know more about what does and doesn't work.

Whew! I told the opening line, the story, and the closing line. I got through it all, and it wasn't so bad. It was fun! What do I do now?

Tell it again! Many storytellers tell a story at least five to ten times before feeling that the story is really theirs. They smooth out parts where they stumble over words, learn to allow for a longer pause for laughter at a particular part, emphasize a passage, or drop a description because it slows the action. They fine-tune the story until it suits them. If you're telling the story to a wall, the wall won't mind hearing it again. If you're telling the story to children, don't worry about boring them. As any parent or teacher can tell you, most children have absolutely no objection to hearing a story told over and over.

As you grow more confident in telling your story, you can start accepting comments. Watch yourself on video or listen to yourself on tape. Encourage the children to talk about their favorite parts. Ask an adult for comments. Practice specific parts if they need work. Tell the story and then tell it again. Soon you'll know it by heart.

Okay. I've smoothed the edges, I've practiced, and I'm ready to share my story!

Wonderful! You've worked hard to get to this point, and your reward is coming soon. But before you call your listeners to gather round, take a look at the site where you'll be telling. You owe it to your listeners and to yourself to make sure that the story will be heard.

What's the shape and size of the room? Can people see you? Can they hear you in the back? Is there a microphone available, and can you get practice time with it? Will there be other activities going on, or will you be the focus of attention? Is there a place for you to set a glass of water in case your throat gets dry? Will the sun be shining directly into your eyes at that time of day? Will the sun be shining into your listeners' eyes? What happens if it rains?

Stories can be told on a stage in front of hundreds of people, but some tellers prefer a more intimate setting. They'd rather tell the same story twice to two small groups. How many people will you be sharing your story with? Is there adequate seating? Are you going to ask people to sit on the floor? On hay bales? On the grass under a tree? Most children think going outside is a special treat,

and telling a story under the open sky makes your storytelling special, too.

Some of these factors may be beyond your control, but by thinking or asking about them beforehand, you won't be caught totally by surprise if something changes.

After you evaluate the site, evaluate yourself. What are you going to wear? If you move about and use your arms, you'll want to wear clothes that don't bind across the shoulders. Look for shirts that won't pop open or come untucked easily. Wear trousers or skirts that let you breathe. Makeup will emphasize your features. Arrange your hair so it doesn't bother you.

Some storytellers like to add an unusual article of clothing that can be taken off later: a hat, a scarf, a cloak, a brightly colored shirt worn over regular clothes. Other storytellers dress in unusual clothing from head to toe. Jewelry can be another distinctive touch, but long dangling earrings may distract people from looking at your face, and a set of bangles or a beaded necklace may make too much noise. A "costume," elaborate or simple, is not necessary, but it does mark you as someone special. It sets the storyteller—and the story—apart from the everyday world and adds excitement and mystery.

The big day has arrived (with a few small problems).

You've practiced your story. You're confident you know how to tell it. You've evaluated the site ahead of time, a glass of water is waiting for you, and all is well as the audience arrives. You're dressed in comfortable clothes of your choice, you're on time, you've visited the restroom, you're waiting to tell your story . . . and your hands are trembling, your heart is pounding, and you feel as if you're going to throw up.

You have stage fright.

This is completely normal, whether you've told one story or one thousand stories, whether your audience is hundreds of people at Carnegie Hall or four preschoolers sitting on carpet squares. Your body is preparing to expend higher amounts of energy during your storytelling, and so your adrenaline level increases, but before you start, that energy has nowhere to go. Don't ignore or try to suppress your heightened awareness and extra energy—use it. If possible, walk around. If that's not possible, tap your feet or clench and unclench your fists. Close your eyes and try to identify all the sounds you hear. Can you distinguish smells? To calm yourself, take deep breaths. Yawn. Not dainty yawns hidden behind your hand, but great jaw-cracking yawns. This both increases your oxygen intake and loosens your vocal cords.

Finally, it is time. The audience is waiting, you move to your storytelling spot, and all are silent, waiting for you to begin. Make eye contact with people in different parts of the room. Smile. If you haven't been introduced by another speaker, say your name now. "Good morning, children. My name is Sara Johnson, and this morning I'm going to share a story with you."

Some storytellers like to engage the audience in dialogue by asking a question, making some comment about the room, or telling a little bit about themselves. If you do this, you must make it clear when the dialogue is over and when the story begins, or the audience will be unsure if they are allowed to comment on the story as it goes along.

A straightforward declaration is often the best, especially for younger children. "Now I'm going to ask you to be quiet while I tell you the story of 'Goldilocks and the Three Bears.'" Then begin, just as you have practiced. If you get unwanted comments during the story, a quiet hush and a finger to the lips may suffice. Maybe a character in a story can say, "It's too loud with all this chattering going on!" and then the character will be happy when the noise subsides. For inveterate chatterers, you may have to stop the story momentarily and say, "There will be time for you to talk later. I'm telling the story now."

Sometimes, though, you want audience participation during a story. Maybe you want them to chant a song to help the sailors hoist the ropes, or clap their hands to make a fairy come back to life. But once that's done, you need to take back the stage. Again, make your expectations clear. "Avast! There's a pirate ship approaching! All hands quiet!"

or "Shhh. She's waking up now. We have to be quiet so we don't scare her."

The story is going along great, your characters are vivid and real, the audience is spellbound . . . and then you forget what to say. You have absolutely no idea what comes next. First, don't lose heart. This happens even to the most experienced of storytellers. Second, sip some water or take a breath. Take two. A pause that seems long and terrifyingly empty to you can seem short and dramatically charged to a listener. Third, if you still can't remember what to say, turn to the audience for help. Ask, "What do you think Goldilocks should do?" or "What do you think happened next?" Their answers, even if you don't agree with them, will remind you of where you are and where you need to go.

But what if you can't get to that place because you've forgotten something important to the story? What if Goldilocks is already upstairs and hasn't eaten any porridge? There are three choices. You can skip the porridge completely, or you can have her go back downstairs and eat it. The third and more difficult choice is to say, "But what had happened earlier was . . ." Flashbacks aren't recommended in storytelling because they often confuse the listeners, but if the information is crucial to the story, you may need one.

All problems solved, you proceed smoothly to the end of your tale, just as you have practiced. You pause after the last line of the story, say your sig-

nature phrase if you have one, then perhaps give a slight bow or look to the floor. When you look back up, your listeners are clapping and smiling, and you feel great! You're shared a story, and shared an important part of yourself. Accept the applause. Acknowledge it with a smile or a wave or another slight bow. Let them give to you as you have given to them.

When story time is over, the storyteller must leave. If you're in a Sunday service, simply returning to your seat will let the minister take over from there. If you're telling your story to a class, you can say goodbye, motion to the teacher to direct the students' attention toward her or him, and leave.

Then give yourself a well-deserved pat on the back. You're a storyteller now!

I've told nursery tales to a religious education class. Now I want to tell a story about Unitarian Universalism.

Great! That's precisely why this book was written. Most of the people in the stories are either Unitarian or Universalist. Those names can be easy to confuse, especially if you're nervous. Writing a small T (for Unitarian) or V (for Universalist) on the palm of your hand can remind you which church they belonged to.

Many of these stories include precise dates, along with descriptions of the era, to help place them in people's minds.

Over two hundred years ago (when the United States of America was still the thirteen colonies), there lived a man named John Murray. . . .

In the city of Prague, in the land of Czechoslovakia, in the year nineteen hundred and twenty-three, a time between the two World Wars, there was a church. . . .

If you find numbers distracting, the year need not be explicitly mentioned. Because of the amount of factual detail, the historical stories may require more preparation time than the folktale-style stories. You may decide that you prefer to read the historical stories aloud instead of learning them as tales, at least for the first few times. For younger classes, some historical details may be omitted. Feel free to adapt the stories so that they work for you.

I love telling stories! I want to learn more.

Storytelling is an art that we develop, and as with all art forms, there is always more to learn. We learn by doing, and nothing can teach you more about your own storytelling than for you to get out there and tell the stories. Different stories, different places, different types of groups, different times of day, different ages . . . each experience will teach you something new.

The essence of storytelling is that it is done live, person to person, with teller and listener looking into each other's eyes. One of the best ways to learn about storytelling is very simple: Listen to storytellers tell their stories. If at all possible, go in person, though listening on tape or watching a video is useful, too. Notice how the storytellers choose their words, how they pause, how they move.

When the performance is over, the storytellers will probably be happy to tell you how they got started and how they've honed their craft. Perhaps they have a group that gathers to practice or to share ideas. Perhaps they know of storytelling workshops you could attend. Classes in storytelling are sometimes offered during UU religious education weekend workshops. All over the world, storytelling festivals are becoming more common.

Finding storytellers near you can be as simple as making a few telephone calls. Schools and libraries often schedule free storytelling programs for a variety of ages. So do some bookstores. Call and ask for the names and schedules of local storytellers. In the United States, the National Storytelling Network (NSN, formerly NAPPS) has a list of members, a bimonthly magazine, conferences, and many storytelling events.

National Storytelling Membership Association
116 West Main Street
Jonesborough, TN 37659
Tel.: 1-800-525-4514; (615) 753-2171
Email: nsn@naxs.net
Web site: www.storynet.org

In Canada, the group Storytellers of Canada/ Conteurs du Canada holds conferences every year in different parts of the country.

Jan Andrews, National Co-ordinator
Storytellers of Canada
R.R. #22230, Lanark ON
Canada, k0g 1k0,
Tel.: (613) 256-0353
Fax: (613) 728-3872

Many other countries and regions have storyteller associations. Once you've found one storyteller, you'll quickly find more.

All of us are linked by the stories we tell. We learn from each other, and we learn about each other through those tales. Stories can make us laugh or cry. They can help us understand another person's pain or move us to political action. A vital part of the interdependent web of all existence is created by tellers spinning yarns and weaving worlds from words.

So be a spinner. Share your stories and help weave a better world.

For Further Reading

STORYTELLING

Creative Storytelling: Choosing, Inventing, and Sharing Tales for Children by Jack Maguire. Cambridge, MA: Yellow Moon Press, 1985.

More helpful tips on storytelling, including how to remember plots, adapt stories to specific circumstances, and add gestures and dramatic voices.

From Long Ago and Many Lands: Stories for Children Told Anew by Sophia Lyon Fahs. Boston: Skinner House Books, 1995.

A wonderful treasury of forty-two tales from around the world and through the ages, plus a chapter with tips on storytelling. (The tales were collected by Sophia Lyon Fahs, who was the editor of children's material for the American Unitarian Association and editor of the Association's Beacon Series of educational books. She was ordained to the Unitarian Universalist ministry in 1959 at the age of eighty-two.)

Improving Your Storytelling: Beyond the Basics for All Who Tell Stories in Work or Play by Doug Lipman. August House, 1999.

Speaks mainly to the experienced storyteller, but don't wait too long to read it. Many of Lipman's exercises and suggestions will be useful to a novice, and they can prevent problems before they start. The book includes tips for body posture and getting "into" a character, breathing and exercise techniques to help deal with stage fright and stress in the vocal cords, and more.

The Storyteller's Start-Up Book: Finding, Learning, Performing, and Using Folktales by Margaret Read MacDonald. Little Rock, AR: August House, 1993.

A thorough and engaging guide to storytelling in front of audiences. Includes twelve tales and specific suggestions for each one.

Tell Me a Story: Creating Bedtime Tales Your Children Will Dream On by Chase Collins. Boston: Houghton Mifflin Company, 1992.

Designed for parents who want to make up stories for their children, this is a delightful and gentle introduction to the art of storytelling.

Telling Our Tales: Stories and Storytelling for All Ages by Jeanette Ross. Boston: Skinner House Books, 2002.

Features thirty-eight stories for audiences of all ages, plus a wealth of ideas for generating new stories on your own or with a group. Each story is accompanied by an outline, performance tips, and a section detailing the origin of the tale. Also includes tips for adapting stories to different age groups, suggestions for props, and performance suggestions.

The Way of the Storyteller by Ruth Sawyer. New York: Penguin Books, 1990.

A classic in the field, first published in 1942, this is a storyteller/librarian's heartfelt account of the spiritual and emotional importance of storytelling, both for the teller and for the listener. Includes breathing exercises, eleven stories, a reading list, and suggestions of where to find more stories.

UNITARIAN UNIVERSALIST HISTORY

Discarded Legacy: Politics and Poetics in the Life of Frances E. W. Harper by Melba Joyce Boyd. Detroit: Wayne State University Press, 1994.

"The Edict of Torda: Religious Tolerance and the Rise of Unitarianism in Transylvania" by David E. Bumbaugh. *Lock Haven International Review* 10, 1996.

"The Feminization of the Unitarian Universalist Clergy: Impacts, Speculations, and Longings" by Dawn Sangrey. *Journal of Liberal Religion* 2:1, 2000.

Lewis Howard Latimer by Glennette Tilly Turner. Englewood Cliffs, NJ: Silver Burdett Press, 1991.

Lewis Latimer by Winifred Latimer Norman and Lily Patterson. New York: Chelsea House Publishers, 1994.

Liberal Religious Feminism: Moving Toward a Gender-Inclusive Religious Community by Carol Hepokoski. Pamphlet published by the Unitarian Universalist Women's Federation, undated.

Norbert Fabian Čapek: A Spiritual Journey by Richard Henry. Boston: Skinner House Books, 1999.

"The Preacher Who Saved California's Soul: Thomas Starr King" by William H. Wingfield. *Real West Magazine*, August 1972.

The Premise & the Promise: The Story of the Unitarian Universalist Association by Warren R. Ross. Boston: Skinner House Books, 2001.

Prophetic Sisterhood: Liberal Women Ministers of the Frontier, 1880–1930 by Cynthia Grant Tucker. Lincoln, NE: Authors Choice, 2000.

Sacred Dimensions of Women's Experience, edited by Elizabeth Dodson Gray. Wellesley, MA: Roundtable Press, 1988.

Unitarian Universalist Women and Religion Movement: The Beginnings, 1977-1981 by Rosemary Matson. Pamphlet published by the Women and Religion Task

Force, Pacific Central District of the Unitarian Universalist Association, 1997.

The Women and Religion Resolution: The First Decade by Lucile S. Longview. Pamphlet published by the Unitarian Universalist Women's Federation, undated.

Unitarian Universalist Curricula

Around the Church, Around the Year: Unitarian Universalism for Children, Kindergarten to Grade 2 by Jan Evans-Tiller. Boston: UUA, 1990.

Singing the Living Tradition. Boston: UUA, 1993.

A Stepping Stone Year: A Program for 8- to 10-Year-Olds by Margaret K. Gooding. Boston: UUA, 1989.

Travel in Time: Unitarian Universalism for Grades 5 and 6 by Lois E. Ecklund. Boston: UUA, 1991.

UU Kids Book by Charlene Brotman et al. Bedford, MA: Brotman-Marshfield, 1989.

We Believe: Learning and Living Our Unitarian Universalist Principles, edited by Ann Fields and Joan Goodwin. Boston: UUA, 1998.

Web Sites

"Dictionary of Unitarian and Universalist Biography," www.uua.org/uuhs/duub

"Unitarian Universalist Women's Heritage Society," www.uuwhs.org

"Unitarian Universalist Historical Society," www.uua.org/uuhs/

Acknowledgments

I would like to thank the following people for their help during the writing of this book:

• the children at the UU Fellowship of Southern Maryland, for listening

• Mary Ann Kelley, Rev. Richard W. Kelley (minister emeritus of Paint Branch UU Church in Adelphi, Maryland), Marianna Nystrom, Dave Reed, Rev. Anne Herndon (minister of the UU Fellowship of Southern Maryland), Fred Burggraf, and Steve Nystrom, for their support

• Lucile Schuck Longview, Carolyn McDade, and Rosemary Matson, for answering many questions about the creation of the Water Ritual

• the friendly and helpful people on the UU History Chat List, most especially Peter Hughes, Rev. Dr. Dorothy May Emerson (executive director of the UU Women's Heritage Society), and KB Inglee; and also Rev. Richard Henry (minister emeritus of First Unitarian Church in Salt Lake City), Michael D. Burp, Michael Masters (assistant director of Murray Grove), Jim Hunt, Jane Hunt, Bonnie Smith, Cathy Tauscher, Charles Grady, Rev. Elinor Artman (minister emerita of Heritage UU Church in Cincinnati, Ohio), Cole Wiggins (president of the Universalist Convocation and publisher of the *Universalist Herald* magazine), and Rev. Anthony P. Johnson (minister of the First UU Church of Essex County in Orange, New Jersey)

• the many people who have posted their essays, sermons, and research on the World Wide Web, making information easy to find, including Rev. Scott W. Alexander, Lee Bluemel, Lisa Doege, Ernest Cassara, Rev. Dorothy Emerson, Suan Karlson, Rev. Suzelle Lynch, Rev. Peter Morales, Laurie Carter Noble, Rev. Dr. Patrick T. O'Neill, and Rev. Harris Riordan

• Tim Berners-Lee, for inventing the World Wide Web in 1989 and making this and many other projects enormously easier

• Mary Benard in the UUA Publications Office, for her patience and encouragement

• Judith Frediani and Marjorie Bowens-Wheatley at Lifespan Faith Development

• Steve, for his patience and love

• Bridget, Vi, Shelley, Tanja, Robin, and MacNair, cyber-sisters and excellent friends, who were there for the beginnings and helped me along the way.